# VISIONARY
# VINE

# VISIONARY VINE

Hallucinogenic Healing in the Peruvian Amazon

# Marlene Dobkin de Rios

*Professor of Anthropology*
*California State University*
*Fullerton, California*

**Waveland Press, Inc.**
Prospect Heights, Illinois

For information about this book, write or call:

Waveland Press, Inc.
P.O. Box 400
Prospect Heights, Illinois 60070
(312) 634-0081

Dedico este libro a los pobres de Belén—resbalando por las calles de sus vidas.

# Contents

Illustrations      ix

Acknowledgments      xi

Map of Peru      1

"Oh Amazonas Putrefacto," by Roger Rumrrill      2

1    Introduction      7

2    Hallucinogens and Altered States of Consciousness      19

3    South American Hallucinogenic Use      37

4  Iquitos: An Ethnography              49

5  Ayahuasca Healing Sessions          67

6  Witchcraft and Illness              77

7  Ayahuasca Healers and Patients:
   Biographies                         99

8  Ayahuasca Visions                  117

9  Mechanisms of Healing              129


   Glossary                           141


   Bibliography                       147


   Index                              157

# Illustrations

A street scene in Belen.    11
The author's house in Belen.    13
A woman nursing her child in Belen.    16
Ayahuasca, the visionary vine.    21
*Visionary drawing.*    27
The mescaline cactus *San Pedro* for sale in a Chiclayo
    marketplace (upper row).    32
*Visionary drawing.*    44
*Visionary drawing.*    52
Approaching Pueblo Libre from Venecia.    60
An ayahuasca healing session in a jungle clearing.    70
*Visionary drawing.*    74
*Visionary drawing.*    80
Fortunetelling cards, locally called *naipes.*    90
An *Ayahuascero*'s house in Belen.    101
*Visionary drawing.*    110
*Visionary drawing.*    119

# Acknowledgments

This book has grown out of a year's research on psychotherapy with aya-huasca (a harmine drink) in Iquitos, Peru, and funded by the Foundations Fund for Research in Psychiatry 67–395 (in collaboration with Oscar Rios Reategui). Needless to say, the data presented in this book are the sole respon-sibility of the author. A deep debt of gratitude is acknowledged to Dr. Carlos Alberto Seguín, former Director of the Institute of Social Psychiatry, National University of San Marcos, Lima, the sponsor of this study. Dr. Seguín's support and continued guidance has made this study a reality.

For a series of practical reasons, this book will present only one part of an ethno-psychiatric collaboration which emerged from a study of folk psycho-therapy with the hallucinogenic vine, ayahuasca. With the publication of Dr. Rios' study of the psychiatric aspects of ayahuasca healing, it is hoped that a multidimensional approach to the mechanisms of "psychedelic" curing will emerge.

A warm *abrazo* of thanks to the many friends in Iquitos is offered for their interest and support in conducting this study. Drs. Varese and Romani, in Lima, were helpful friends and colleagues in difficult moments of analysis. A debt of gratitude, as well, is acknowledged to Dr. Frits Wils for his exhaustive study of Belén and its importance to the present work. Thanks, too, are in order to Dr. Frank Adams and Dr. Marion Kilson for their reading of earlier drafts of this book and their helpful comments. A small grant from the Cali-fornia State College at Fullerton Foundation has aided greatly in preparation of the final draft of this book for publication.

Thanks are due to the Office of Academic Programs, the Smithsonian Institution, during the summer of 1970, for making available its facilities to the author in readying a final draft of this book.

A longer version of the materials on the *naipes* has appeared in the *Journal of American Folklore,* Volume 82, No. 324, April-June, 1969, under the title, "Fortune's Malice: Divination, Psychotherapy and Folk Medicine in Peru." Grateful acknowledgment is made to the editor of the journal for permission to reproduce part of the article.

Finally, sincere thanks to my husband, Yando, for his insightful comments and suggestions.

Marlene Dobkin de Rios

*Fullerton, California*

# VISIONARY
# VINE

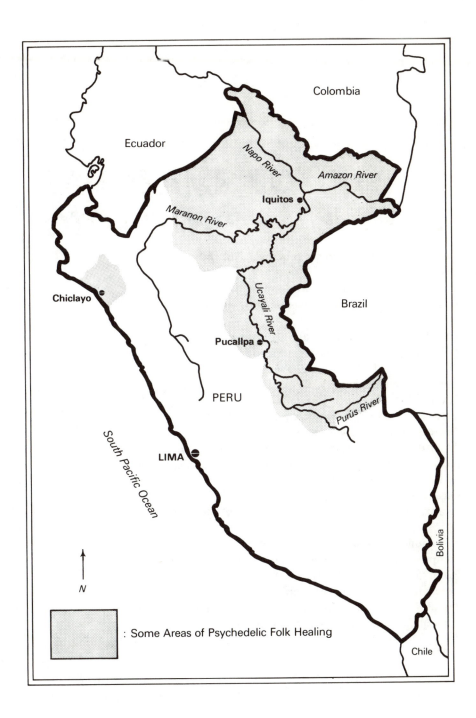

: Some Areas of Psychedelic Folk Healing

# OH AMAZONAS PUTREFACTO

Como un pez hinchado y expuesto al Sol
navego el Amazonas.
En mi retina guardo el último horizonte
y el turbio sabor de tus aguas putrefactas en mi boca.
Oh Amazonas,
yo solo veo en tu história al viejo y tuerto capitan
gritando a su tropilla hambrienta:
"Ea soldados de España, ea, avancemos hacía el Sur."
Cubierto de patrañas
navego de horizonte a horizonte.
Vetustos pueblos queman sus piltrafas al Sol.
"Ea españoles, ea, avancemos."
La tarde cubrese de un negro resplandor de gallinazos y
pequeñas mujeres de arcilla queman los últimos secretos
de su sexo en las hogueras.
Oh Amazonas putrefacto.
Avanzo por las calcinadas o las del día y me pregunto:
¿Por que morir entre tus aguas?
Yo renuncio a tu voz
e impreco por tus antiguos mitos, tus amores turbios.
Recorro desde el Sur al Norte
los caminos que otros hollaron pero
descubro viejas mentiras que cubrieron con musgo las edades
y los quejidos de pueblos que han olvidado su memoria.

# OH, PUTREFIED AMAZONAS

As a fish, swollen and exposed to the sun,
I sail the Amazonas.
I keep before me the last horizon I saw,
And the turbid taste of your putrefied waters in my mouth.
Oh, Amazonas,
I only see in your history the old and one-eyed captain,
Shouting to his ravenous crew:
"Ay, soldiers of Spain, ay, let's move on to the south."
Full of exaggerated, untrue stories,
I sail from horizon to horizon.
Forgotten towns burn their scraps in the sun.
"Ay, Spaniards, ay, let's move on."
The late afternoon is covered with a blackened splendor of vultures and
Small, clay-colored women burn with the secrets of their sex as if on fire.
Oh, putrefied Amazonas,
I advance through the calcined waves of the day and wonder:
Why die in your waters?
I reject your voice
And evoke your ancient myths, your unhappy loves.
I travel from north to south
The roads that others have tread, but
I discover old lies that, like musk, have covered the ages,
And the moans of towns that have forgotten your memory.

Oh Amazonas,
como un pez hinchado y putrefacto
navego por tus aguas
y mastico el tiempo
que ahogose en tu corriente, en tus sucias turbiedades de ramera
de vieja bruja enmohecida por los años.
Aguí queda, Amazonas, tu única história
expuesta al Sol como esos peces que se tuestan al atardecer,
tu piel lamida por pestilentes ahogados
en las noches que navegan fantásmas y caucheros
recogiendo las últimas monedas dejadas por el día.
Oh Amazonas, solo guardo de ti el último desfile fantasmal
de pueblos y viejas edades sepultas en tu vientre.

Roger Rumrrill

Oh, Amazonas,
As a fish swollen and putrefied,
I sail your waters
And ruminate on time,
Which drowns in your current, in your filthy turbidness of the
Whorish old witch moldy with age.
Here, Amazonas, remains your only history
Exposed to the sun like those fish which are being dried at twilight,
Your skin licked by the pestilence of drowning
In the nights that phantasms and rubber gatherers sail,
Gathering the last coins left by the day.
Oh, Amazonas, your only memory for me is the last parade of
Spectres of towns and old times entombed in your belly.

translated by Marlene Dobkin de Rios

# Introduction

If we followed the Atlantic Ocean west past the mouth of the Amazon River to travel some 2300 miles inland, we would pass through the monotonous, verdant rain forests of Brazil and Colombia, eventually arriving at a sleepy Peruvian city called Iquitos. High on an eroding palisade adorned with turn-of-the-century Eiffel-designed houses, imported ceramic tiles, and paved streets, the city stands in stark contrast to the hundreds of villages we passed in our Amazon journey. Iquitos is full of cement splendors which contrast enormously to the floating community of Belén, in the southeastern section of the city, set upon balsa rafts.

Belén and parts of Iquitos share a jungle heritage with hundreds of other hamlets radiating out in all directions. These areas are places where the hallucinogenic vine, ayahuasca, is made into a drink that is used in sessions to treat illness, effect love magic, and bewitch. Mostly, the plant is used in healing sessions, where it is taken by patients and healers alike in isolated jungle clearings at the edge of the city.

The visions induced by the drug are interpreted by a healer to help patients gain insight into the reason they are ill. In this part of the world, where people believe that illness comes about not from natural causes but as the result of some kind of magic, the powerful psychedelic plays an important role in the revelation of evil-doing. Poor people are not the only ones who look to a healer for help. Men and women of middle-class mien and background, expensively dressed bank administrators and high army officials, as well as the poor, seek in the drink a last resort in their search to be cured.

One August evening in 1968, along with six other people, I was seated around a circle in an open area some miles on the outskirts of Iquitos. I listened attentively to a tall, lean, middle-aged man, who was simply dressed. He whistled melodies unlike any I had ever heard, as he passed a plastic cup around the circle. Filled with an unpleasant-smelling drink, the cup containing the ayahuasca potion was handed to each man and woman by Don José, after he carefully blew tobacco smoke over it. As the evening passed, the man walked around the circle, addressing each person individually as he shook a leafy rattle to accompany his healing incantations. I sat quietly throughout the evening, trying to understand my first ayahuasca session. What was going on? Nothing at all dramatic seemed to be happening. A group of people dressed in cotton dresses or inexpensively made slacks and shirts were sitting in a circle in an out-of-the-way place. A man methodically went about his business of whistling, singing, and blowing tobacco smoke over their heads and bodies in turn. As an anthropologist who had been funded to study psychedelic healing in this quiet little Amazonian city, I was observing my first ayahuasca session because of the kindness of the healer, whom I had met only some days before. He was recommended to me by a psychiatrist with whom I had worked in Lima. Dr. Chiappe visited Iquitos some months before to obtain the powerful plants for animal experimentation. We were both affiliated with the Institute of Social Psychiatry, part of the National University of San Marcos in Lima. Dr. Carlos Alberto Seguín, as Director of the Institute, supported the study on the use of ayahuasca in Iquitos psychotherapy. Various psychiatrists, psychologists, social workers, and now myself, an anthropologist, were all interested in the rich natural laboratory that Peru presented, as mind-altering plants like ayahuasca have been used for many centuries in healing activities.

The summer before, in 1967, I worked with the Institute for three months in a north coastal village some 500 miles outside of Lima. I was part of an interdisciplinary team whose purpose was to study the use of a mescaline cactus, called San Pedro, as it was used in ritual healing (see Dobkin de Rios 1969b, 1968). Prior to my 1967 study and for a total of two years, I prepared for the ayahuasca project by reading almost everything in French, Spanish, and English that I could get hold of concerning the *Banisteriopsis* vine. Ayahuasca, the vine of the spirits, as the liana was called, was said to cause fast-moving visions, somatic changes, and perceptual alterations. How difficult it was that first night, watching those men and women take the drug, to fathom what was going on. In fact, until I, myself, took ayahuasca some months later, I felt entirely like an objective observer who was at best only able to record the vaguest outlines of a phenomenon which defied description. It was obvious to me, even in these early months of field work, that the totality of the drug experiences I was observing went well beyond the sum of the particulars I might write up in my little notebook late that night, when after each session I returned to the city.

Without fully realizing it at the time, I was far too much like the many travelers, botanists, missionaries, and ethnographers who, with some notable exceptions in different parts of the world, had found themselves living among people who used powerful mind-altering plants for various reasons, yet who were unable to understand or even recognize the worlds of altered consciousness caused by such plants. Cultural blinders of some sort or other hampered many of these observers, who were Westerners in thought and perceptions. At best, they might describe minute details of the externals of drug-using ceremonies, reaching their pinnacle of accuracy perhaps when they had to analyze alcohol-based rituals and ceremonies. Without doubt, their own culturally determined fears of testing potent brews (I was similarly fearful during initial months of research) closed off a world of subjective activity which their informants may have hinted at only barely in the most carefully structured interview or questionnaire.

For too many years, such inner states had been off-limits to psychological investigation, which focused its attention on mental activity that was measurable and objectively discernible. Since interior states were not amenable to available measurement techniques, they were often disregarded. However, it is in just those areas of hallucinogenic-drug use that measurement of subjective states becomes an almost impossible task. Despite the subjective nature of a drug experience, what would appear to be the most important aspect of my ayahuasca research was to see how cultural variables such as belief systems, attitudes, expectations, and values concerning the use of a powerful psychedelic plant can structure one of the most personal experiences that a social scientist can examine. Recurrent features and regularities of individuals' drug experiences in the Peruvian Amazon will be an important part of the analysis in the pages to follow.

My own study in Iquitos was centered in the urban slum of Belén. It was general knowledge that healers and patients could be found in large number in this community of some 12,000 people. Nonetheless, interest in ayahuasca was by no means limited to poorer sections of the city, such as Belén. Throughout the year that I lived in Iquitos, I visited other sections of the city. Conversations would often turn to the subject of interesting plants like ayahuasca, and tales would be told of friends or relatives of well-to-do and educated people who had been cured or bewitched through ayahuasca use.

When I first arrived in Iquitos, I was unable to find housing in the slum because of overcrowded conditions. As a result, I rented a small house in the city itself about a mile away from Belén, and spent the first six months visiting the community. I quickly made friends with a tiny woman, doña Felicia, whose small, floating house was moored precariously on a bank near a path that led to the waterfront area. Felicia allowed me to use her house to prepare meals, rest from the midday heat, and receive guests. I became very friendly with her two grown daughters, who were valuable informants, especially in the areas of love magic. They generally introduced me to life in the community and, at times, accompanied me on visits to other houses.

My initial impressions of Belén the first days were hard to sort out. The first response of viewing the slum as a homogeneous area gave way to finer distinctions, despite the overwhelming visual onslaught of a helter-skelter arrangement of houses, canoes, and rafts. People moved about, buying and selling produce that arrived in small, wooden boats called *colectivos*. Women and children manned small stalls where food was offered for sale. Incredible smells of floating sewage assaulted the senses. My first day in Belén was spent in the company of a lawyer from the Regional University of Iquitos, who introduced me to various shopkeepers and people he knew from the time that he and several of his students conducted a sociological study of the community some four years prior to my arrival.

In the days that followed, I visited Belén with a young university student. We rented a little canoe to visit some inaccessible areas of the community in an inundated section of the slum. Through these first encounters, we saw the three named segments of Belén take shape. The upper section, called Belén, is still within the city confines. It straddles the largest of the three urban markets. This section of the city benefits from electricity, piped water, and adequate sewage. Houses are like other city dwellings, with wooden walls and calamine roofs. As you walk down the endless steps going toward the river (perhaps the equivalent of six city blocks), you reach a section called Venecia. It is named after the Italian city, Venice, because of its flooded appearance some four months of the year. Venecia's main plaza during most of the year serves as a popular meeting place. One of the community's two primary schools faces the square and is where dances are held on Saturday nights. They are organized by an association of heads of families in Belén, who try to raise money for various activities. Continuing, one finally approaches a series of inlet canals that are naturally flooded at different times of the year, and are docking sites for produce-laden jungle craft. Crossing over the first canal on vine-lashed balsa logs, you reach the farthest end of Belén, called Pueblo Libre. As I walked toward Pueblo Libre from the higher city areas those first days, the quality of life seemed to me to deteriorate. Houses were literally falling apart. Many had walls missing, badly thatched roofs, and inadequate sewage. With increasing distance, one left far behind the sole water fountain available to this population of over 12,000 people.

Once arrangements were made with Felicia to use her house, I set to work earnestly. I remember my difficulties in the first five or six weeks, when it seemed that the only things people would talk to me about were how much

A street scene in Belén.

rice cost, the price of bananas, or just how much the river had risen that morning. Once in a while, I thought I caught innuendos about important things, but although my Spanish was excellent, it was no match for the many Indian words that were part of the rain-forest vocabulary. No doubt, to most of the families with whom I chatted, I was something of an enigma. An unmarried person alone doesn't seem to fit very well into any recognizable human unit. Although initially I had the assistance of a young student from the Regional University, that turned out to be more of a problem than it was worth. Unfortunately, the girl didn't enjoy listening to people, and we spent most of our time talking about her thoughts and activities of the night before, as well as trivia of one sort or another. Most of our informants would listen politely and look away in the distance. When she had to travel for family reasons, a difficult problem was resolved. So I wandered alone through the slum, at times in the company of one of Felicia's daughters but mostly on my own.

My early contacts with women in Belén found me in conversations whose subject invariably returned to me. Although I was rarely asked directly why

I was in Belén, chats in those early months focused on such things as how old I was, how was it that I looked so young for my age (I was 29 at the time), and how it must have been because I wasn't married and suffering from mistreatment by some man. Then, some recipe or ritual would be offered to me, although there was never any indication that it was meant to help me find a man magically. I was very touched, in fact, by my new friends' offers of what they no doubt felt they could best help me with, in an area that they thought I needed advice—namely, how to get and keep a man. Although with time the quantity of love-magic advice diminished, it never entirely stopped filling my evening jottings as I relaxed at home from the rigors of incessant visiting.

As time passed, particular skills I had developed in an earlier visit to Peru in 1967 became of practical use (see Dobkin de Rios, 1969c). My studies of fortune-telling cards, which locally were called *naipes,* enabled me to set up a small consultation office in Felicia's house in January 1969 and to receive clients who were anxious to have their cards read. During the months prior to my official debut as fortuneteller, I brought the cards down to Belén with me one day. During the hot afternoon, I sat with Juana in her mother's house and casually took the cards out of my bag to see her reaction. She was very excited about my ability to read them, even though all the data were carefully indexed on coffee-stained 2 x 2 index cards. She herself spent whatever money she could get her hands on to have her cards read by a dwarf, an old woman who lived in the center of town. My card-reading ability, garnered from little booklets available throughout market places in Peru, albeit clumsy at first, was highly esteemed by Juana and all her friends. For the next few months, I would amuse them by telling fortunes, without, however, taking any money for my time or energy. People who were interested in having their fortunes read didn't take me very seriously at first, since practically nothing exists in Belén without a price tag attached. In January, when Juana's mother Felicia left Belén to work as a laborer in a distant community, I was able to take care of her house. It was then that I began to get a reputation in the slum as a *curiosa,* a fortuneteller who was not only knowledgeable about the future, but who charged a mere pittance for her services. By this time and with the advice of a senior colleague, I decided to charge one Peruvian *sol,* worth about two and one-half cents, or the price of an ice cream that a mother might buy for her youngster. Although I had misgivings initially about the ethics of such a procedure, whatever funds I earned this way went to pay for food and medicine which I gave as gifts to the many people with whom I interacted. My nearest competitors lived in the city itself, a long distance away and charged at least fifteen Peruvian *soles,* the price of a kilo of rice. The feedback I received was that charging for my services was necessary to make the fortune come out correctly. In this way, I was able to cross-check data on belief systems, illness, disease etiology, and the like with my clients. During the year I worked in

Belén, I was able to make friends as I wandered through the slum community in the company of neighbors and friends, attending festivals and funerals. During the day, I was able to receive anxious clients who wished to know what the future held in store for them. Toward the end of my stay, I was able to administer psychological tests to make a comparison with the more than 200 card readings of the *naipes* (see Dobkin de Rios, 1971). In all, having an acceptable social role in Belén made it easy for me, still a young woman in the eyes of my informants, to fit comfortably into the community.

The author's house in Belén.

By late January, the normal ten-minute walk from the bridge linking Venecia to my house in Pueblo Libre would take me from a half hour to an hour and a half. No matter which path I took and what short cuts I tried, people stopped me constantly to ask me to please read their fortunes. One lady, running to catch up with me one late afternoon, apologized for accosting me in the street, but in lieu of introduction said that she had heard "I was the gringa who knew things . . ."

One of the things I had to learn quickly was that brandishing a camera and snapping pictures of daily life was not such a good idea, especially in those first few months when I was new to slum life. A friend of Felicia used to come down to the house to do her washing and indirectly hinted that someone had tried to take a photograph of her once to use against her in bewitchment rituals. Although she made no reference to my own use of a camera, I realized that some people might indeed interpret my photographing in an unkindly light. As a result, I put my camera in a drawer for some four months, until I was asked to take photographs at the funeral of a man whose family I knew. Taking advantage of the several camera shops in Iquitos that could quickly develop black-and-white prints, I began to give away prints to those people who permitted me to use the camera. The role of "town photographer" was very useful, since I was invited to many festivals and funerals in Pueblo Libre. People were fairly sure they could depend on me to give them photographs a few days later.

Since my study was organized around the topic of ayahuasca use, I set about gathering information not only on the way of life of the people of Belén, but in particular on their beliefs about illness and the role of the powerful plant hallucinogen in their society. I remember quite clearly how I decided in the early days of my study that I would not be the first to mention the name of the plant. Indeed, it wasn't long at all before my new friends began to ask me if anything like ayahuasca existed in my own country. Each new day brought notes full of ayahuasca use. Soon, one family that I had befriended introduced me to a healer, don Carlos, who was treating the mother of the household. The family invited me to attend an ayahuasca session, since I had an automobile available and could help bring the patient home late at night. In this way, working among a "normal population" of ayahuasca users, I was able systematically to gather data on beliefs, values, and expectations concerning the plant's use, as well as to make friends with several ayahuasca healers and their families.

One such contact, with don Antonio, developed into a deep friendship. In October, after having observed some half-dozen ayahuasca sessions, he agreed to invite me to try the vine myself. Many evenings at his house after he had finished seeing patients who came to him with health problems, we would talk at length about his patients and the nature of their illnesses.

Occasionally, friends from Belén would invite me to accompany them to their jungle hamlets where they grew up. We would journey by boat anywhere from several hours to a day or so, either in a privately owned motorized canoe or in one of the many *colectivos* (ferries) that connected Iquitos to small jungle villages. In this way, I was able to get a perspective on both urban and rural dimensions of drug healing and syndromes of illness.

One trip which enabled me to appreciate the quality of life in rural areas as compared to the overcrowded conditions in Belén occurred when a young woman invited me to go along with her husband Victor, their children, and her to witness a soccer match in her husband's village. One afternoon at about 4 P.M. approximately fifteen people, including most of the Belén team, loaded into a long canoe with an outboard motor. We rode all night, stopping off at a few hamlets along the way, since it was Saturday night and some of the young people wanted to dance at local festivities and enjoy themselves. At dawn, we arrived at Victor's hamlet. After beaching the canoe, we slipped and slid with our gear in the twenty-minute walk to our destination. The path leading from the dock to the house was eerie in the morning stillness, as the rain forest presented a canopy of trees with little light penetrating the walkway, still slippery from recent rains. The whole scene had a surrealistic flavor to it. We came to the house which stood alone in a clearing. Stumps of burnt trees and tomato patches surrounded it. Victor's mother was friendly and received me warmly, but all I cared about was getting some sleep. I stretched out on the floor, since hammocks were a rarity, and rested for a few hours before the morning's activities began. Unfortunately, our soccer team from Belén didn't win the match, but then, they must have been as tired as I was from the night's journey and revelry.

There was no ayahuasca healer in that immediate village with whom I was able to visit. Nonetheless, the change of pace was welcomed, as life in the countryside was quiet, friendly, tranquil. Mind you, there was no ready cash available for the many people whose leached lands rarely gave them more than one or two harvests before they had to clear other intractable areas of jungle to get a harvest. Yet at least they had land to sustain them, quite a contrast to almost three-quarters of the population in Belén, who had to make odd jobs do to obtain the means to live.

In a way, I was fortunate that I was not the first to study the community of Belén. Since it was so vast an area, and I was only one person, it would have been impossible to have covered all of the areas with equal ease. Most of my time was spent walking around Pueblo Libre and talking to neighbors and strangers who rarely, if ever, refused to speak to me. During the four years prior to my fieldwork, various sociological surveys of the community and Iquitos had been made, and a large amount of statistical data was available to me in published form. Thus, I was able to use traditional anthropological techniques of participant observation as if I were working in a small community and cross-check my data against the statistical tables and norms that others before me had determined.

In two surveys, the populations questioned in Belén represented larger percentages of households than one normally finds in such sociological studies. The best of the four studies, completed in 1967 by Wils, examined over 106 families out of the 1000 officially licensed to utilize state land for their houses, or some 10% of the total. Another study, completed in 1964, utilized 300 families in the community, or roughly 30% of the total (Oviedo, *et al.*). One of the least useful of the three focusing upon Belén, also completed in 1964 by Grajeda, used 663 families, or over 66% of the total. The fourth study available, once again, was done by Wils in 1968 on the city of Iquitos. A small but representative sample of 553 interviewees were used while attempts were made to control for geographic dispersement and markers of social stratification.

A woman nursing her child in Belén.

Although most of my own forays kept me in Pueblo Libre, several of the healers I knew lived in Venecia and other parts of the city, so that in a general manner I was able to interview people from various sections of the city.

Perhaps the highlight of my year's work came one night when I accompanied Felicia to a spiritualist healing session in a neighboring house. Although ayahuasca was not going to be used in the ceremony, one of the healer's friends, Stéfano, had the reputation of occasionally using the plant to heal. Stéfano didn't like me very much. At times, when he was drunk, he shouted insults at me as I would pass his house. That night he was quite inebriated. When Felicia and I arrived, we took seats and smiled at the people who were there, almost all of whom we knew. Stéfano turned to Felicia and said loudly, "Why did you bring the gringa?" Felicia, who is a good twelve inches shorter than I, didn't answer for a moment. Hugging me, she said, "She is my daughter." I giggled nervously, and Stéfano made an obscene remark, indicating that if I were Felicia's daughter, he was her son-in-law. We all drank huge amounts of aguardiente that burned as it went down, and the awkward moment passed. But I did feel that I had managed to fit in, that my anxieties and fears about my work and my relationships with the people of Belén had somehow arranged themselves comfortably.

When the year's study of the visionary vine came to an end, I returned to the United States to take up a teaching position in California. This period marked another important step in organizing my data, as I tried to learn as much as possible about plant hallucinogens, their chemistry, and how they were used in other non-Western societies.

In this book, my own study of ayahuasca will be presented within a broader framework of hallucinogenic-plant use. A cross-cultural focus on mind-altering plants and the history of ayahuasca use in the South American Amazon region should set the stage for a more detailed analysis of the way in which this powerful liana has served man for both good and evil ends.

# Hallucinogens and Altered States of Consciousness

2

Chemical substances used to alter states of consciousness have a long and hallowed use in human history, although many people are unaware of the antiquity of hallucinogenic plants which have been tried in teas, drinks, brews, snuffs, and also smoked to bring about mental and physical changes. Yet there is evidence from archaeological remains, oral tradition, current primitive practices, ancient chroniclers, and heroic sagas which attest to the fact that man—unlike most if not all of his relatives in the animal kingdom—has a certain fascination with inducing non-ordinary states of reality.

These mind-manifesting substances which are popularly knows as "psychedelics" have been used throughout the world since the beginning of recorded time and perhaps even much earlier. They have been used for both good and evil—to heal, to bewitch, to prophesy, and to entertain. They have provided man with a means to achieve divine guidance, to provide a transcendental thrill as a source of religious activity, to provide solace in situations of distressing culture change, and for therapeutic benefit in healing situations (Ludwig, 1969:19).

One such plant about which very little is known is ayahuasca. A woody jungle liana that grows in the tropical rain forests of Peru, Colombia, Ecuador, and Brazil, this vine has a long history among primitive groups,[1] as well as among present-day Mestizo men and women who use the hallucinogenic vine in folk medi-

---

[1]See chapter three for a detailed discussion of primitive ayahuasca use.

cine. Belonging to various botanical species of *Banisteriopsis*,[2] its principal alkaloids are harmine, harmaline, and tetrahydroharmine. Ayahuasca is one of the lesser-known mind expanders, as powerful in its effects as LSD and mescaline.

Despite the spate of popular books and articles that have appeared in recent years on various hallucinogenic drugs,[3] few have realistically considered these substances from a cultural point of view—examining the way in which they have been utilized in one way or another in different societies. The anthropologist can offer an analysis of the cultural dimension of hallucinogenic use in primitive and peasant society by showing the way in which such substances have been used in relating man to nature, healing his ills, entertaining, diverting, and edifying him.

This book will focus in particular upon ayahuasca, a visionary vine. Its long history and relative unfamiliarity to most should provide insight into a time-honored tradition of psychedelic curing.

Since the 1950s, many of these substances found in nature or synthesized in laboratories have found their way into modern psychiatric practice. A huge literature on the use of LSD alone exists in the field of psychology, pointing up two major ways in which medical practitioners have used such substances either in short-range or long-term treatment of psychoneurotic disorders (see Caldwell, 1968). Since the latter part of the 1960s, however, with growing problems of runaway drug use among young people in Western Europe and the United States, the use of such drugs in psychotherapy and basic research has been drastically curtailed. For this reason, an examination of the traditional use of hallucinogens such as ayahuasca in South American societies becomes all the more pertinent as a means of understanding the potential adaptive value of psychedelics.

### What Are Hallucinogens?

Before beginning a comparative journey through deserts, high mountains, rain forest, and open plains in order to examine the host of over forty species of hallucinogenic plants found in South America that cause alterations in consciousness (see Schultes, 1965), it might be wise to define hallucinogenic substances more carefully as well as to consider how they affect man.

The type of drug that the popular term psychedelic encompasses is only one of the three major categories of "psychotropic" substances. The properties of such psychotropic substances cause psychological changes or modify mental

---

[2]Including *B. caapi, B. inebrians, B. quitensis, B. rusbyana.*
[3]See in particular Friedberg (1965), Masters and Houston (1966), LaBarre (1964), Caldwell (1968), Efron (1967), Tart (1969), Abramson (1967), Blum (1969).

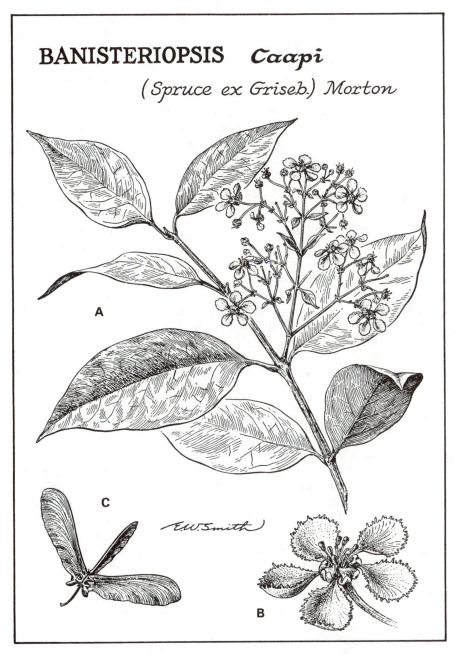

# BANISTERIOPSIS *Caapi*
## *(Spruce ex Griseb.) Morton*

A. Flowering branch, about ½ x. B. Fruit, somewhat larger than ½ x. C. Flower, about 2½ x. **(Reproduced by permission of the Botanical Museum, Harvard University, from** Harvard University Botanical Museum Leaflets**, vol. 18, no. 1, June 1957.)**

activity either when the plant form or an artificial synthesis is used. The French psychopharmacologist Delay (1967: 2) has distinguished three major types of psychotropic drugs. The first group includes psychic sedatives such as the narcotics, barbiturates, and tranquilizers and other drugs which are used extensively in modern psychiatric practice (including, for example, the pheno-thiazines). Psychic stimulants such as the amines, which are drugs of mood change, are the second important group. Finally, the psychic deviators (which are often called hallucinogens), like mescaline, LSD, psilocybin, and aya-huasca, are a category with great importance in the anthropological record. Hallucinogens, unlike the first group, do not cause physical addiction.

### How Ayahuasca and Other LSD-Type Substances Affect Man

Harmine, one of the major alkaloids found in ayahuasca, is an indole hallucinogen derived from native plant materials. LSD-like substances such as harmine have a complex chemistry and pharmacology. Certainly the shaman throughout the primitive world knows nothing formal about the way in which his sacred plants perform, except by empirical observations. We, too, know little about harmine's action on the body; however, there is one aspect of the drug's chemistry that we can mention.

An important component of ayahuasca is an indole ring.

N
H

The same ring is also found in serotonin (5-hydroxytryptamine), a chemical very important in the workings of the human central nervous system, which may possibly transmit nerve impulses (Barber, 1970:11). The exact relation-ship of indole substances and serotonin antagonism, however, is not yet clear and still remains to be delineated. There may be interference with the proper functioning of natural substances whose turnover is basic for normal brain functioning (Hoffer, *et al.,* 1967:472, 502).

LSD-like substances without doubt interfere with the transmission of stimuli from one cell to another in the nervous system, either at the synapse or by altering cellular activity. As Hoffer points out (*ibid.,* 211), either could lead to marked change in brain function. In addition to the chemical activity of a drug, the actual drug experience or "trip" is never simply reducible to a pure chemical effect. Many other variables such as how the drug is adminis-tered and by whom, the emotional atmosphere, the presence or absence of music, the individual's mood, personality attributes, expectation, etc.: all enter the picture. Dosage level, too, must be considered. Although hallucinogenic drugs are considered to be drugs of awareness and rarely cause "hallucinations" in the sense that the individual lacks comprehension of his surroundings, nonetheless very high dosage levels can drastically modify the sense of external reality.

Various writers have shown that chemical substances are by no means the only way that man has attempted to vary the pace of everyday life. Exercises, meditation, fasting, flagellation, hypnosis, trance phenomena induced by rhythmic dancing, musical chants, and other activities readily spring to mind as means of achieving a different phenomenal reality. Whatever the value of such methods, hallucinogenic drugs for the most part have been a much quicker way to achieve states of altered consciousness, requiring less concentration or preparation than other cultural customs that have developed throughout human history. For example, one anthropologist has written about trance phenomena among the Ga women of Ghana, in which provoked behavior required long periods of training on the part of young women, most probably at a subliminal level, before some mystical communication with a protective spirit was achievable (Kilson, 1968: 68). Certainly the use of chemical substances in different societies often necessitates special preparations or settings. Shamans may have to go through extensive apprenticeship periods. Nonetheless, if we compare psychedelic-drug use to yoga techniques which also aim at changing consciousness at will over a period of long years of training, it is clear that drugs can definitely hasten this process of mental alteration.

The work done by Arnold Ludwig on altered states of consciousness is most helpful in a discussion such as this. His ideas will be introduced again in subsequent chapters dealing with ayahuasca. Ludwig has examined the many different ways that man uses to alter his states of waking consciousness, and has delineated the following ten general characteristics (most of which apply to hallucinogens in one degree or other):

1. Alterations in Thinking: At a subjective level, varying disturbances in concentration, attention, memory, and judgment occur, with a possible decrease in reflective awareness.

2. Disturbed Time Sense: The sense of time and chronology alters with perhaps a person feeling a sense of timelessness, or else time may be experienced as either slowing down or accelerating. Time may also seem to be infinite or unbelievably short in its duration.

3. Loss of Control: A person may show an initial fear of losing his grip on reality or else losing his self-control. He may offer some resistance to experiencing an altered state of consciousness. However, a person may willingly want to enter this state, especially if cultural beliefs exist which

hold that one can experience divinity or become a mouthpiece for a god(s) through such activity.

4. Change in Emotional Expression: Unlike normal emotional expression during waking hours, a person may display emotional extremes ranging in degree from ecstasy and orgiastic equivalents to profound fear and depression.

5. Changes in Body Image: Various distortions in bodily image are frequently reported. Many individuals experience a profound sense of depersonalization, or some schism between body and mind, such as a feeling of the dissolution of boundaries between one's self and others, the world, or the universe. These body changes may be regarded during the drug state as strange and even frightening. Spontaneous experiences of dizziness, blurring of vision, numbness, and analgesia may also be found.

6. Perceptual Distortions: Increased visual imagery, hyperacuteness of perceptions, and illusions of different varieties are found. Many factors may be influential here, including cultural expectations, individual or wish-fulfillment fantasies, as well as geometric patterns in differing colors, shapes, and forms. Hallucinogenic drugs can often bring forth a phenomenon known as synesthesia when a certain scrambling of sensory modalities occurs: thus, one may see what one hears.

7. Change in Meaning or Significance: Many people have a predilection to attach special significance to their subjective experience, ideas, or perceptions. Great insight or profound feelings of meaning may follow such experiences.

8. Sense of the Ineffable: After entering such states, a difficulty in communicating the nature or essence of the experience to someone uninitiated may be felt.

9. Feelings of Rejuvenation: Many people claim to have experienced a new sense of hope, rejuvenation, or rebirth at the termination of the experience.

10. Hypersuggestibility: There is increased susceptibility and the propensity of persons to uncritically accept or respond to specific statements, or nonspecific cues (in particular, cultural expectations for certain types of behavior or subjective feelings). A person, especially when undergoing a psychedelic experience, may feel the need to seek support or guidance to relieve some of the anxiety associated with loss of control, and may therefore rely more on the suggestions of the person who is guiding him through the session (Ludwig, 1969: 13–16).

As Ludwig shows, altered states of consciousness have various functions in human societies. Their ubiquitous presence in one form or another bears witness to their importance and their ability to satisfy both individual and social needs (p. 18). Ludwig notes that various altered states of consciousness may be maladaptive as well as adaptive to man. In a maladaptive sense, such changes may bring on depersonalization and dissociative states, acute psychotic and panic reactions, escape from responsibilities and inner tensions, or the symbolic acting out of unconscious conflicts. At a primitive or peasant level, some substances are intricately tied to a magical world view and on occasion used in witchcraft and sorcery activities by evildoers. Needless to say, anxiety levels can have frightening consequences in an over-all mental-health sense (see Kennedy, 1970). On the other hand, adaptive expressions can be important too, as man attempts to resolve psychic tensions or relieve conflict without endangering himself or others. Drug-adjuncted folk healing through-out human history is but one example of harnessing altered states of conscious-ness to beneficial use. Induction of such states is part and parcel of many psychological therapies used by shamans and folk healers throughout human societies. In many cases, entering an altered state of consciousness may be seen by a particular group as essential for receiving communication with a spirit or deity, something which is viewed as absolutely necessary to ensure that healing takes place.

Another area of adaptation that Ludwig identifies is the avenue of new realms of experience that open to man. New knowledge, inspiration, and religious, revelatory, or prophetic insights can be gained in this manner. Moral values may become affirmed, emotional conflicts may be resolved, and coping with human predicaments and the world outside may be eased. Further, the aesthetic experience that a person can gain from a psychedelic experience may broaden his subjective sensitivities and serve as a source of inspiration. In group settings, altered states of consciousness fulfill both individual and group needs. Religious ceremonies enable a group representative to achieve commun-ion with a deity, to divine the future, or to create a sense of security and omnipotence "in the face of the despair and hopelessness of a marginal exis-tence" (Ludwig, 1969:21).

In contemporary American society, there is no doubt that both the legal and illegal aspects of hallucinogenic-drug use contrast dramatically with societies where hallucinogens have a long historical tradition. Calling upon comparative materials to aid in understanding one's own culture is a pastime many an-thropologists including myself find not only difficult to resist but useful in obtaining a perspective on such pressing social concerns as the present "drug question" in industrial societies. To dismiss psychedelic-drug use as danger-ous, evil, and immoral, or as a problem necessitating stricter legislation and law enforcement in order to better control or eliminate such use, only mirrors what we can call a hallucinophobic world view. Given the puritan ethic which still permeates our society, it is easy enough to understand how altering states of consciousness is legally limited to our traditional substances of tobacco and alcohol. Both are pernicious and proven health hazards to their users. Just as the Wassons (1957) would see the world's people divided into mushroom lovers and mushroom haters, so too could one view particular cultures as hallucinophilic or hallucinophobic. The latter phenomenon no doubt is derived from the Judeo-Christian tradition with its great disdain for pleasure or sensual enjoyment. With inadequate data available on the longitudinal effects of many if not most psychedelic substances, as well as culturally accepted drugs such as tranquilizers, barbiturates, and amphetamines, the anthropological record assumes even greater importance as a control. While some societies such as those in Peru have thousands of years of hallucinogenic tradition behind them, advanced industrial societies often find themselves in deep trouble as segments of their society are suddenly discovering the use of powerful mind-altering substances.

To elaborate, in Peru and in other parts of the world, evidence would seem to indicate several thousand years of plant-hallucinogenic use (see Dobkin de Rios, 1969b). Historical sources such as the Veddic hymns of India and the Homeric epics of Greece tell of the use of plants and other natural substances to alter states of consciousness. Such use has formed the basis of religious belief and sacramental rites as well as of social activity. Stopping at the historical records is premature: we might try to speculate a bit and push the evidence back in time still further, perhaps to as long ago as half a million years, when man first learned to use fire. Human evolutionary studies indicate that the crucial factors in man's evolution have been the development of upright posture and increased brain size. As man evolved from lower orders and his posture became upright, the amount of land area available to him for foraging increased immensely and was one of the major keys to his evolutionary success. We might postulate that some of the various plants with which he experimented in his omnivorous search for food might at times have been psychotropic in their effects. The second evolutionary factor mentioned above—larger brain size and increased awareness—is also of paramount importance in explaining how relatively puny, canineless creatures who weighed less than 100 pounds could manage to survive in the hostile, predator-filled environments in which they existed in South and East Africa some two million years ago or more. We might speculate further as to the stimulation of language and communication in the wake of such plant usage, as the desire to convey information about nonordinary states of reality following the ingestion of such plants might have occurred (see Wasson and Wasson, 1957: 154). It was not, however, until the advent of fire, and in particular the process of boiling (either by means of hot stones dropped into woven fiber baskets or until the use of ceramics or gourds for cooking was known) that many hallucinogenic plants could be converted into a chemical state where their mind-manifesting properties could be activated. Many plant hallucinogens need to be pulverized, boiled long

hours, or smoked to release their special properties. Such is indeed the case with the ayahuasca vine[4] to be discussed in this book.

Weston La Barre, the eminent anthropologist who has devoted much of his academic life to the study of peyote use among North American Indian groups, has commented upon the antiquity of New World drug use. Hunters and gatherers, rather than farming peoples, interestingly enough, might in his opinion have been the ones to learn the properties of hallucinogenic flora in their environments, especially since these peoples were more often under hunger pressures to experiment with potential foodstuffs than their Neolithic descendants, who were abundantly supplied with both staple cultigens and domesticated animals (La Barre, 1970: 73). Since more than 95% of man's history was spent as hunter or gatherer, the implications for the long periods of time in which such plants may have been known and used are important to consider.

## The History of Certain Psychotropic Plants

Although detailed studies of the history of psychotropic-drug use have already been made,[5] a quick summation of man's use of some mind-altering substances does cause the unsuspecting reader to pull himself up sharply and wonder indeed at the hiatus in his knowledge. Far too few of us realize that we live in a sea of chemicals in our own society, where alcohol, tranquilizers, nicotine, caffeine, amphetamines, barbiturates, aspirins, and many other drugs are used in large quantities and have become an integral part of the "American Way of Life" (Barber, 1970: 84). One should also keep in mind that socially approved drugs may not necessarily be good for individuals merely because they are legal. Look, for example, at alcohol and tobacco, which can and do cause grave physical harm. The increasing amount of evidence linking tobacco smoking to lung cancer is as disturbing as the statistics concerning the millions of people in the United States, for example, who are alcoholics and must seek relief from publicly supported medical and counseling facilities (see Fort, 1969: 112).

When we realize that the use of drugs in our own society is quite irrational in that we hardly limit ourselves to drugs of proven worth, it becomes easier to suspend our cultural blinders concerning drug use in other parts of the world. However, delving into the dimensions of drug use in different cultures presents various possibilities of ordering and systematizing the mountains of data so as to understand the adaptive and maladaptive aspects of drug use. We

---

[4]The vine is generally cut into small pieces and boiled four to six hours until a syrupy liquid is obtained.

[5]See, for example, Taylor (1966) and Blum (1969).

could look first at particular culture areas and whatever drugs happen to fall within geographical-ecological regions. Or, we could group the data together according to a particular plant. Perhaps we would prefer to place different societies together according to some sort of evolutionary criteria. A fourth possibility is a thematic approach, seeking some common denominator in order to link together drug use in distinct cultures of the world which would make sense to the reader unsophisticated in the intricacies of material treating hallucinogens and culture.

A thematic approach, of course, suffers from the danger of dissecting drug use from a holistic setting. After all, many drugs have been used by the same people in a variety of ways throughout time. However, arranging the data according to theme need not entail wrenching such materials out of social context. I believe that certain themes pertaining to drug use can be delineated from the empirical data and for purposes of analysis can be compressed into three major headings. The first group we will deal with, "Drugs and the Supernatural," points up man's use of such substances for magical-religious ends, to divine the future, and to orient him in his search for good or evil. A second category, "Drugs and the Treatment of Disease," although intricately linked to cosmological beliefs and supernatural philosophies of causation in many primitive and peasant societies, still presents a meaningful cognitive category for the Western reader. Drug therapies (like that of ayahuasca, the main concern of this book) are greatly diffused in time and space and present the reader with some new materials. Finally, the third category, "Drugs, Pleasure, and Social Interaction," links together general areas of drug use as reported in scattered societies of the world.

## Drugs and the Supernatural

Although a great many examples could be selected here,[6] a few representative studies will be chosen to illustrate how some plants have played extremely important roles in man's life. One scholar, Gordon Wasson (1957), has written a provocative account of the important role that widespread hallucinogenic mushrooms (the fungi of various forest trees such as the birch and fir) must have had in the development of supernatural beliefs in early man. Whether or not we agree with his thesis that the ubiquity of belief systems concerning the supernatural is due to man's primordial encounter with mind-altering plants, nonetheless the worlds of heaven and hell opened to man by the visionary content of such infusions may have played an important part in stimulating his mythologies and legends concerning otherworldly lands and peoples, de-

---

[6]See Dobkin de Rios, in press, for a survey of hallucinogenic-drug use among non-Western cultures.

mons, devils, and the like. As mentioned earlier, Wasson has viewed the peoples of the world as either mycophobic or mycophiliac; that is, they either adore or detest mushrooms. When the mushrooms in question are hallucinogenic (and there are well over twenty species in Mexico alone), then complications set in. Siberian shamans of reindeer-hunting communities are believed to have used the colorful fly agaric mushroom to enter into a world where the soul could be separated from the body. The mushrooms were gathered during a short season when their quantity was very limited. Only older men were permitted to ingest the plant, but others, too, were able to partake of the religious experience by means of a clever solution devised very early in their history. Drinking the urine of a man who had ingested the powerful visionary plant permitted a second and then a third person to alter his state of consciousness. From man to man, thus, urine was passed around the community; in fact, it was stated in early reports that some of the unpleasant bodily side-effects of the fly agaric mushroom, such as nausea and vomiting, were minimized as the substance passed through a person's body: the second time around was much less bothersome in this manner.

In Mexico, near the mountains of Oaxaca, the Mazatec Indians have been using a variety of hallucinogenic mushrooms (including the genus *Psilocybe mexicana*) for uncountable decades. Despite the fact that the Spanish were heavily mycophobic in their response to such plant use, the Mazatecs continued their use of the plant secretly for four hundred years. Men and women who ingest the mushrooms say that the god of the plant speaks to them and advises them about their affairs or prophesies the future. In some villages, the plant is used in connection with Roman Catholic liturgy, to ensure abundant crops.

The well-known Aztecs of Central Mexico, were no strangers to the use of mind-altering plants in religious ritual. The early Spanish chroniclers mentioned the use of *ololiuqui,* the vision-inducing morning-glory plant. Although the majority of the chroniclers were priests who inveighed against the plants they called "diabolic seed," the people they observed esteemed the plant as a divine messenger which was capable of transporting man's mind to spirit realms (Schultes, 1969: 349). One priest, José de Acosta, in 1590 observed the Mexican use of what he called the "abominable unction which the Mexican priests and other nations used and of their witchcraft." The plants involved in the ritual included *petun,* a species of tobacco which was mixed together with venomous spiders, scorpions, salamanders, and vipers. Young boys gathered these creatures, burnt them at the temple hearth, and mixed the ashes to obtain visions or to offer before statues of their gods. Acosta wrote that the use of this ointment permitted shamans to speak with the devil. Sacrifices, too, were linked to the supposed cruelty that the drug caused in men's hearts (Acosta, 1590; cited in Brooks, 1937:1590).

The Aztecs also used *teonanactl*, believed to be intoxicating mushrooms, which they called the "Flesh of the Gods." Church persecution against the hated pagan custom drove this cult into hiding for four centuries. Hernandez, an early chronicler, wrote in 1790 of the three kinds of hallucinogenic mushrooms worshipped by the natives, some of which he wrote "cause not death but madness that on occasion is lasting, of which one symptom is a kind of uncontrolled laughter . . . there are others again which, without inducing laughter, bring before the eyes all kinds of things, such as wars and the likeness of kings. Yet others there are not less desired by princes for their festivals and banquets, and these fetch a high price. With night-vigils are they sought, awesome and terrifying" (cited in Schultes, 1969: 350). The coronation of Montezuma, observed by a Spaniard in 1502, reported the following use of hallucinogenic plants:

. . . to strangers they gave wild mushrooms to eat in order to intoxicate them, after which they began to dance. The sacrifice over, they marched to the temple, with the court bathed in human blood; there they ate uncooked mushrooms, nourishment which made them lose all their senses and left them in a worse state than if they had taken a lot of wine. They were so drunk and lacking reason that many committed suicide, and thanks to the power of the mushrooms, they had visions and the future was revealed to them, and the devil spoke to them while they were in this drunken state (Durand, quoted in Heim, 1969: 203).

Mushrooms are not the only mind-altering plants that have been incorporated into religious ritual. Tobacco, an Old World plant, was believed to have been used in North America as early as A.D. 200 possibly in connection with rain-making rituals (Blum, 1969: 87). A very little known African plant, *Iboga,* found especially in Gabon and adjacent parts of the Congo, was reported by French and Belgian explorers in the middle of the nineteenth century to be used in a variety of ways (see Pope, 1969). Some tribal groups discovered that large doses of the plant would induce visual hallucinations, and the plant was incorporated into initiation rites for secret cults. Guien has described the use of this plant in the *Bwiti* or *Bouiti* rites where a complicated ceremony and tribal dance involving the use of the plant permit the initiate to obtain a vision of the *Bwiti* spirit. Shamans took the drug to find out information from the spirit world or seek advice from ancestors (Schultes, 1970: 36).

### Drugs and the Treatment of Disease

One of the most interesting ways in which psychotropic plants have been used by man is in the treatment of disease. I don't say here in the *cure* of disease, because as yet very little is known about the chemistry of such substances and their effects on man. As one old sage has put it, "Nature cures the disease while the healer amuses the patient." Although many plants could be

The mescaline cactus **San Pedro** for sale in a Chiclayo marketplace (upper row).

cited in this context, one particular plant about which little is known is a mescaline cactus, long, spineless, and rigid, called in Spanish *San Pedro,* used on the dry desert coast of Peru and Ecuador. During the summer of 1967, I was able to study the use of this plant in folk medicine in a small Peruvian agricultural village on the north coast.[7] In a land of rich agricuotural potential, spotted with small farming villages operating in relationship to market centers on the relatively industrialized Peruvian coast, the use of this cactus can be traced back through thousands of years to a distant past when it played an important role in pre-Incaic civilizations, finding its way into ceramic artistic

---

[7]See Dobkin de Rios (1968).

representations. Today, men and women specialized in the art of healing gather together small groups of patients who take a drink made from boiling the cactus many hours. Seated in open farmlands, some distance from their home, a healer utilizes a complex ritual blended with Roman Catholic liturgy, prayers, relics of saints, as well as a series of magical items such as polished stones, mineral chunks, ancient ceramic pots, and polished sticks in a table *(mesa)* set with his ritual charms and protection. The ritual itself consists of special songs and whistling, activities believed efficacious to extricate evil afflicting a patient, and a faith in the spirits controlled by the healer and called up under his mescaline visions. The cactus, one sample of which contained 1.29 grams of mescaline per kilogram of fresh materials, is by no means the only psychotropic plant the healer uses. In addition, various datura plants (a powerful hallucinogenic-plant group) are mixed together in the boiling process for extra strength. In this particular Peruvian community (I've called it by a pseudonym, Valleseco) over one hundred men and women are reputed to specialize in the use of the plant to treat emotionally and psychologically precipitated illness, whose causation is linked to a system of beliefs in evildoing on the part of spirits of nature or by evil-minded people. The use of this plant attracts people to this community from all over Peru.

Another plant which we colloquially call marijuana in the United States— the *Cannabis sativa* plant of the Middle East—also has a long history of medical use at village-level society throughout areas of North Africa, India, Egypt, and Iran. Ancient Ayurveda and Unani Tibbi medical systems have been using parts of this plant for over ten centuries in treating a series of diseases. Some of the plant's uses have been to promote appetite and digestion, heal stomach pains, bind the bowels, and create antiphlegmatic states, or as an aphrodisiac or in constipation disorders. Some 500,000 Ayurvedic practitioners scattered in as many small villages use this plant in healing and are valued members of their rural communities (see Dwarakanath, 1965: 16–18).

Still another psychotropic plant used like the mescaline cactus of Peru is peyote, a small, spineless cactus which is one of the most ancient sacred hallucinogens of Mexico. Early commentators wrote with amazement about the properties of this vision-inducing plant which spread from its area of origin in northern Mexico to numerous North American Indian groups who currently use the plant as part of religious ritual in the Native American Church. Although peyote-cult members use the plant for a variety of reasons, including communication with the supernatural, many peyote meetings are held to heal the sick. Early reports of the plant's therapeutic role mentioned its external use on wounds. Walkington and other botanists found in 1960 that peyote possessed antibiotic properties. The plant's ingestion for its hallucinogenic properties was rather late, then, compared to this original use. Plant users believe that peyote teaches, and in cases of mental illness, cult members say that the plant enables them to have access to supernatural power, which can be used to overcome illness or misfortune. Diagnosing the cause of illness, too, is thought possible through the use of this plant. For some North American Indian groups, such as the Navaho, it provides security against two of the most anxiety-provoking features of traditional values, namely witches and ghosts (see McGlothlin, 1967: 10).

## Drugs, Pleasure, and Social Interaction

While in Western society such drugs as alcohol and tobacco generally afford the user relaxation, pleasure, relief from tension, or provide ease in casual encounters, other societies have institutionalized distinctive stimulants, narcotics, and hallucinogens in a similar manner. Peru, once again, presents us with some excellent material on coca use, a plant stimulant that has served for fortification against the elements and to facilitate social interaction on the part of highland Andean Indians who must often walk long distances over hilly mountains with insufficient nourishment. The coca leaf, mixed with a ball of lime, enables the man or woman chewing a wad in his mouth to endure long hours of activity with little discomfort.

Like their Andean counterparts, food gatherers in the Central Australian desert, traditionally used the pituri plant *(Duboisia hopwoodii)* to facilitate traveling long distances with little water or food. Little is known about the plant or its use except that it did play a prominent role in the totemic ceremonies of some aboriginal groups as well. When the English penetrated the interior regions of Australia, they found an area naturally desolate, lacking food and water. Some aborigines gave the Australian scientist Joseph King pituri, which probably saved his life. Although the aborigines are a nomadic people with a simple culture, their inhospitable land of scrub vegetation possesses the important pituri plant. Its benefits were such to the aborigines that trade routes and migrations, called pituri roads, were very widespread, and reports state that some natives walked over 400 miles to obtain the plant. Containing the alkaloid scopolamine (formerly used as the "twilight sleep" anesthesia), pituri has toxic properties which can cause the death of animals such as the emu in the Australian desert. It is also used to poison fish without endangering the person eating the fish, but its most dramatic effects are upon man himself, especially in its ability to kill fatigue and reduce hunger and the need for water (Taylor, 1966: 152–156).

A hallucinogenic snuff *(Virola theiodora)*, called *epená* by certain Venezuelan Indian groups, is prepared from a red bark resin of a forest tree. Widely used in northwestern Brazil and nearby Colombia and Venezuela, virola intoxication varies but usually includes increased excitability, numbness of the limbs, nausea, visual hallucinations, and at times a disturbed sleep. Although there is some ritual use of the plant by medicine men in Colombian groups, this doesn't seem to be the case among the Waika Indians of Venezuela. Nor is there any formal motivation for taking the snuff. One casual observer, Seitz, mentioned the obvious enjoyment received by the Indians who went into a dance and sang as the effects of the snuff were felt. It appears that prior to European contact, the drug was used more extensively to enter into communication with a world of spirit beings, called *Hakula* spirits (Seitz, 1967: 334).

In the next chapter, we will look at one area of the world, namely South America, where plant hallucinogens have been highly elaborated in native societies. An intensive regional study using the same typology of drug use should be an interesting backdrop to the ayahuasca materials.

# South American Hallucinogenic Use

3

The vast array of data concerning the use of plant hallucinogens in non-Western society illustrates very clearly that these substances have been used in such diverse cultural activities as magic and religion, healing, divination, pleasure-seeking, and witchcraft. In Tables 3:1–3:3, a selected list of the use of various plants has been arranged in accordance with their social function in over fifteen South American societies. Our three major categories will illustrate the incorporation of particular hallucinogenic substances into important areas of cultural activity. No attempt has been made to relate such drug use to other cultural variables within a statistical framework. When such a task was attempted by Blum in 1969, he found that analyzing data from the Human Relations Area File was futile. He found that not only did ethnographers, travelers, and other observers pay little attention to drug use among the people they visited, but that when they did report on such behavior, they were notoriously unreliable in their findings. Blum found few drugs in the Human Relations Area File for which adequate descriptions existed and a real lack of cultural data that could be related to drug use (1969: 140–141). It is hoped that the following detailed analysis, both historical and contemporary, of ayahuasca use in the Peruvian Amazon will remedy some of the kinds of hallucinogenic "ethnographic deserts" that Blum and others have encountered.

Although Tables 3:1–3:3 make no pretense of being a complete record of South American hallucinogenic

TABLE 3:1. HALLUCINOGENS AND THE SUPERNATURAL

A. MAGICAL-RELIGIOUS USES

| CULTURAL USE | SOCIETY, LOCATION | TYPE OF PLANT SUBSTANCE | BOTANICAL NAME AND/OR VERNACULAR | BIBLIOGRAPHIC REFERENCE |
|---|---|---|---|---|
| Divine guidance and communication with gods; divine contact with spirit world | 1. Jivaro, Ecuador | woody vine | var. *Banisteriopsis* sps. natéma (Jivaro) ayahuasca (Quechua) | Karsten, 1935: 432–436 |
| | 2. Kariri & Pankararu Indians, Brazil | root | *mimosa hostilis* vinho de jurema (Portuguese) | Schultes, 1967: 42 Sietz, 1967: 317 |
| | 3. Yanomamo Indians Venezuela & Brazil | snuffs | *Virola theiodora* epená | Chagnon, 1968: 52 |
| To achieve trance states | 1. Chibca, Colombia | | borrachero (*ipomea carnea?*) | Naranjo, 1968: 6 |
| | 2. Chocos, Colombia | | huantuc (*datura sanguinea*) | *Ibid.* |
| | 3. Quechuas, Bolivia | | chamico (*datura stramonium*) | *Ibid.* |
| | 4. Mapuche-Huilliches, Chile | barks, seeds, and leaves of various datura plants | Var. *datura* sps. floripondio (Spanish) campanilla (Spanish) | Cooper, 1949: 555–7 *Ibid.* |
| | 5. Zaparos, Ecuador | | huacacachua (Quechua) yerba de huaca (Spanish) | Cooper, *loc. cit.* |
| | 6. Amazon and Orinoco rain forest tribes such as Jivaros, Canelos, Piojes, Omáguas, etc. | | huanto (Spanish) miaya maikomo tonga | *Ibid.* *Ibid.* *Ibid.* *Ibid.* |
| | 7. Inganos | | pej | *Ibid.* |
| | 8. Sioans | | isshiona | Schultes, 1970: 46 |
| Training of prospective shaman | 1. Mestizos, Peruvian Amazon | woody vine | var. *Banisteriopsis* sps. ayahuasca (Quechua) | Dobkin de Rios: this work. |
| | 2. Goajiro, Colombia | hallucinogenic tobacco(?) | *Nicotiana tobacum*(?) Manilla (vernacular) | Giraldo, 1950: 20 |

**B. DIVINATION**

| CULTURAL USE | SOCIETY, LOCATION | TYPE OF PLANT SUBSTANCE | BOTANICAL NAME AND/OR VERNACULAR | BIBLIOGRAPHIC REFERENCE |
|---|---|---|---|---|
| Induce dreams so as to see the future | Zaparo, Ecuador<br><br>Amazonian Indian groups | woody vine | var. *Banisteriopsis* sps. | Reinburg, 1921: 31<br><br>Masters, 1966: 114–5 |
| Prophecy | Jivaro, E. Ecuador | woody vine | *Banisteriopsis caapi* (*natema* - Jivaro) (*ayahuasca* - Quechua) | Karsten, 1935: 123–4 |
| | Jivaro, E. Ecuador | leaves of a bush | *Datura arborea* (*maikoa* - Jivaro) (*huantuc* - Quechua) | Karsten, 1923: 72–73 |
| Telepathic agent; clairvoyance | Orinoco river basin horticultural groups, Colombia, Venezuela; Jivaro, Ecuador | leaves | *Ilex. sp* (*guayusa* - vernacular) | Karsten, 1935: 174, 380 |
| Discover whereabouts of a missing person | Goajiro, Colombia | Hallucinogenic tobacco(?) | *Nicotiana tabacum*(?) | Bolinder, 1957: 130–6 |
| Induce intoxication to fortell the future and through communication with the devil | Inca, Andean region | Snuff made from seeds and pods, mixed with chicha | *Piptadenia peregrina* cohoba, vilca, yopo snuff. | Schultes, 1969: 345 |

C. WITCHCRAFT

| CULTURAL USE | SOCIETY, LOCATION | TYPE OF PLANT SUBSTANCE | BOTANICAL NAME AND/OR VERNACULAR | BIBLIOGRAPHIC REFERENCE |
|---|---|---|---|---|
| Cause illness to another through psychic or physical means | Jivaro, Ecuador<br><br>Peruvian Amazonian Mestizo groups<br>Araucanian Indians, Chile | woody vine<br><br>woody vine<br><br>spiny shrub | *Banisteriopsis* sps.<br>(*ayahuasca* - Quechua)<br>(*natema* - Jivaro)<br>*Banisteriopsis* sps.<br>(*ayahuasca* - Quechua)<br>*Latua pubiflora*<br>*arbol de los brujos* | Harner, 1968<br><br>Dobkin de Rios:<br>this work<br>Schultes, 1970: 48 |
| Capture identity of another for harm | Ecuadorian and Peruvian Mestizos, coastal | cactus (spineless) | *Trichocereus pachanoi*<br>(*San Pedro* - Spanish) | Gutiérrez Noriega, 1950 |
| Send mountain demons to enemy villages to eat skulls of children | Yanomamo, Brazil and Venezuela | snuff from tree bark | *Virola Theiodora*<br>(*epená* - vernacular) | Seitz, 1967: 317<br>Chagnon, 1968: 109<br>Schultes, 1969: 346 |
| Preventative agent against evil malice of people | Omagau Indians, Peru<br>Peruvian Mestizo group, rain forest | woody vine<br><br>hallucinogenic tobacco(?) | *Banisteriopsis* sps.<br>(*ayahuasca* - Quechua)<br>*Nicotiana tabacum*(?) | Girard, 1958: 183<br>Dobkin de Rios:<br>this work |

TABLE 3:2. HALLUCINOGENS AND THE TREATMENT OF DISEASE

| CULTURAL USE | SOCIETY, LOCATION | TYPE OF PLANT SUBSTANCE | BOTANICAL NAME AND/OR VERNACULAR | BIBLIOGRAPHIC REFERENCE |
|---|---|---|---|---|
| Diagnostic: visions used for prescribing remedies | Peruvian coastal, high-land and jungle Mestizo populations | cactus (spineless) | *Trichocereus pachanoi* (*San Pedro* - Spanish) | Dobkin de Rios, 1968 |
| | | tuber | *Datura arborea* (*misha* - vernacular) | Friedberg, 1959: 439 Dobkin de Rios, 1968 Del Castillo, 1963 Lemlij, 1965 |
| | var. *Banisteriopsis* sps. | woody vine | (*ayahuasca* - Quechua) | |
| Identify evil-doer or agent responsible for illness | Peruvian jungle Mestizos | woody vine | *Banisteriopsis* sps. (*ayahuasca* - Quechua) | Dobkin de Rios: this work |
| | Amazonian horticultural groups, Peru, Ecuador, Colombia, Venezuela | woody vine | *Banisteriopsis* sps. (*ayahuasca* - Quechua) | Karsten, 1935: 430 |
| Discover cause of illness | Yanomamo, Venezuela and Brazil | snuff from tree bark | *Virola theiodora* (*epená* - vernacular) | Chagnon, 1968: 109 Seitz, 1967: 317 Schultes, 1969: 346 |
| Anti-spasmodic and analgesic powers | Amazonian horticultural groups | leaves | *Datura suaveneolens* (*toé* - Spanish) (*chamico* - Spanish) | Naranjo, 1968: 6 |
| Anti-diuretic and anti-rheumatic (for snake bites and yellow fever) | Bolivia, Ecuador, Colombian and Brazilian Amazonian horticultural groups | various *Datura* and *solanaceous* plants | *Brunfelsia hopeana* (*sanango* - Spanish) | Schultes, 1957: 44 Schultes, 1970: 43 |
| Invoking of spirits to heal | Goajiro, Colombia | hallucinogenic tobacco(?) | *Nicotiana tabacum*(?) (*manilla* - vernacular) | Giraldo, 1950: 20 |

Table 3:3. Hallucinogens, Pleasure and Social Interaction

| Cultural Use | Society, Location | Type of Plant Substance | Botanical Name and/or Vernacular | Bibliographic Reference |
|---|---|---|---|---|
| To achieve ecstacy, pleasurable or intoxicated state | Cubeo, Colombia | woody vine | *Banisteriopsis* sps. (*mihi* - vernacular) (*ayahuasca* - Quechua) | Goldman, 1963: 210 |
| | Zaparo, Ecuador | woody vine | *Banisteriopsis* sps. (*ayahuasca* - Quechua) | Reinburg, 1921: 31 |
| | Yanomamo, Brazil | snuff from tree bark | *Virola theiodora* (*epená* - vernacular) | Seitz, 1967: 317 |
| Periodic pleasurable effects | Peruvian urban Mestizo populations | woody vine | *Banisteriopsis* sps. (*ayahuasca* - Quechua) | Dobkin de Rios: this work |

use, the general overview from published reports does clarify particular traditions that historically have been associated with the use of mind-altering substances. Of the three major categories, only one seems particularly problematic and nonadaptive in the sense of impeding man's ability to relate to his environment either culturally or psychologically. This is the use of hallucinogens for witchcraft. In chapter six, data on witches who use ayahuasca for evil purposes will be examined in more detail, but it is clear in the writings of many anthropologists who have worked in societies with highly elaborated witchcraft beliefs that anxiety levels, stress, and general duress can be an overwhelming aspect of everyday life (see Kennedy, 1970; Evans-Pritchard, 1937). Insofar as some potent plant substance is believed part of a conjurer's kit, then maladaptive aspects of drug use should not be ignored.

A word here is necessary about another potential maladaptive dimension of plant hallucinogenic use; namely longitudinal health dangers to populations where such plants are frequently employed. Although few if any long-range studies have been done throughout the world, the anthropological data can give us some clues. Much of the material in this book comes from my work with healers—mature men and women who have been using powerful plant hallucinogens on the average of two or three times a week for over periods of years, up to twenty years. Historical evidence for continued hallucinogen use in Peru should provide us with some additional basis for reflection and questions on the potential dangers of such substances.

## Primitive Use of Ayahuasca

The jungles of western South America, which are drained by the upper Amazon tributaries and include parts of modern-day Ecuador, Colombia, Brazil, and Peru, are an area of the world where anthropologists have commented on the use of ayahuasca as an hallucinogenic drink used by primitive horticultural societies. The drink bears the same name as the vine, although various names such as *natema, yajé, yagé, nepe* and *kahi* have been used throughout the basin area. Ayahuasca is the general term that has been applied to several different species of *Banisteriopsis,* to which additional psychedelics may occasionally be added (see Schultes, 1970). Early nineteenth-century travelers and botanists have written with awe of the proliferation of plants used to give exciting and pleasurable effects to many South American primitive horticultural groups.

The inhabitants of the warm lowland Amazonian tropical forest share many cultural traits such as thatched houses, hammocks, dugout canoes, and pottery; they subsist on fish and other animal life in the rivers; they cultivate root crops such as manioc and yucca and have simple village-type societies which

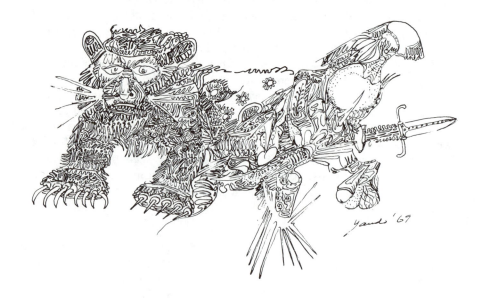

lack any occupational specialization or social differentiation (Lowie, 1949: 4). Nonetheless, their pharmacopoeia of hallucinogenic plants is remarkably elaborated (Steward *et al.,* 1959:284).

Hosts of different uses have been attributed to the visionary vine, ayahuasca. A brief summary of the literature, using the same categories as presented in the tables earlier in this chapter, shows the following ways in which ayahuasca has been incorporated into tropical rain forest activities:

I. Ayahuasca and the Supernatural
   a. For Magic and Religious Ritual: To receive divine guidance and communication with the spirits animating the plants; to receive a special protective spirit (Karsten, 1935: 432–436, 1923: 72–73; Harner, 1962: 181; Schultes, 1957: 74; Cooper, 1949: 552; Spruce, 1908: 416).
   b. In Divination: To tell if strangers were coming; to learn the whereabouts of enemies and to discover their plans; to see if wives were unfaithful; to prophesy the future clearly (Villavicencio, 1858, cited in Schultes, 1963: 147; Spruce, 1908: 424; Reinburg, 1921: 31; Roessner, 1946: 174; Schultes, 1957: 75; Karsten, 1935: 123–124, 1923: 72–73).
   c. In Witchcraft: To cause illness to another through psychic means; to use as a preventative agent against the malice of others (Harner, 1968: 29, 1962: 493; Girard, 1958: 183; Reinburg, 1921: 31; Spruce, 1908: 424).
II. Ayahuasca and the Treatment of Disease: To determine the cause and/or to effect a cure for disease (Reinburg, 1921: 31; Karsten, 1923: 73; Barret, 1932: 310; Spruce, 1908: 416; Perez de Barradas, 1950: 65; Whiffen, 1915: 187; Koch-Grunberg, 1908: 65; Harner, 1968: 28; Siskind, 1970: 9).
III. Ayahuasca, Pleasure, and Social Interaction: To effect pleasurable or aphrodisical states, enhancement of sexual activity, to achieve ecstasy or an intoxicated state; to facilitate social interaction among men (Reinburg, 1921: 31; Whiffen, 1915: 187; Goldman, 1963: 210; Siskind, 1970: personal communication).

Some of the early reports are interesting to read in detail. For example, the French anthropologist, Reinburg, visited the Ecuadorian Zaparo in 1912 and observed the nocturnal use of ayahuasca. Men who would take the drink would avoid certain foods for a two week period: "The Zaparos use ayahuasca to give themselves dreams or to obtain insight into the future. Apparitions in the form of forest dwellers such as tigers, snakes, animals they have known, enemies of neighboring tribes appear to them. They never fail to drink before going out on an expedition. Some take ayahuasca for its own sake, but most use it for sorcery" (1921: 31).

Among the Jivaro Indians of Eastern Ecuador, ayahuasca is used during a

*Tsanta* feast, in which a person who wishes to kill a specific enemy was believed able to acquire an *arutam* soul as protection against physical violence (Harner 1962: 493). Among a Tupi-Guarani group called the Omagua, located near San Joaquin and San Salvador, Peru, Girard mentions the use of ayahuasca by their medicine man as a powerful antidote against what he called "the evil of people." The liana was believed to have the power to produce delirium, hallucinations and sleep (1958: 183).

> In the course of the night, the young men partook of Caapi five or six times in the intervals between the dances, but only a few of them at a time, and very few drank of it twice. In two minutes or less after drinking it, its effects began to be apparent. The Indians turned a deadly pale, trembled in every limb and horror was in his aspect. Suddenly contrary symptoms succeeded. He bursts into a perspiration and seems possessed with reckless fury, seizes whatever arms are at hand, his *muruou,* his bow and arrows . . . and rushes to the doorway where he inflicts violent blows on the ground or the doorposts, calling out all the while, "thus I would do to mine enemy" (Spruce, 1908: 416).

Among the Zaparo and other Indian groups, the "dead man's vine," as ayahuasca has been called, was used as a stimulant at feasts when a medicine man was called upon to settle a dispute or quarrel, to give a proper answer to the representative of another group, or to discover the plans of an enemy. If a man were sick, the drink was used to discover who it was that had bewitched him (*Ibid:* 424). Reinburg has described the use of ayahuasca among the Zaparo for medical purposes. The healer falls into a deep sleep during which time he learns the nature of his patient's illness, which he believes is revealed to him by the spirits that he controls. When he wakes up, he begins to heal by sucking upon the affected area of the patient's body, to bring forth a *chonta* —a small thistle or spine symbolically representing an evil spirit which first he carefully and secretly hid in his mouth. It is believed that the *chonta* is the cause of the illness sent by some enemy (1921: 31).

In 1923, Karsten wrote of the use of ayahuasca (called *natema*) which was used by Ecuadorian Jivaro: "The object of the drinking of the *natema* at the *Tsanta* feast is to find out whether everything will turn out favorably for the slayer in the future; whether he will have a long life, attain to material prosperity and be lucky in his undertakings. . . . At the same time, the persons who have drunk in the sacred drink will be benefited for their own part, also being purified from impure and disease bringing matters and gaining strength and ability for their respective works and occupations" (1923: 72–73).

Religious ideas connected to ayahuasca use have also been discussed by Karsten, who noted that visual illusions which followed in the wake of the ayahuasca experience were ascribed to demons that were believed to animate the plants with whom the Indians said they had intimate contact while under the influence of their medicine. These demons were believed to be ancestral spirits or souls which were transmitted to the plants. The shaman or witch sought the assistance of these creatures to permit them either to cure diseases or else to send away such illness by witchcraft (*Ibid.:* 74).

A more recent study of ayahuasca use among the Sharanahua of the Purus River region (near the Peruvian-Brazilian border) shows that healing is one of the major uses to which ayahuasca is put by the group. To quote: "The most powerful means of curing is the treatment of the shaman, who takes ayahuasca and sings the illness away. When other medicines fail and the person "wants to die," only a shaman can cure him. Of the twenty-five men at Marcos, three are shamans. They are respected and slightly feared, since they are able to make someone sick as well as to cure him" (Siskind 1972: 9). A shaman who was one of Dr. Siskind's informants treated some twenty-seven cases in recent times in which he took ayahuasca for at least half of them.

Compared to these early accounts of ayahuasca use, present-day Mestizo healing with the vine has undergone some major transformations. In the rain forest, secluded Indian tribes took ayahuasca in ritual feasts or else limited its use to shaman. This has virtually disappeared in the city activities (Friedberg 1965: 104). Yet, in spite of the superficial blending of twentieth-century medicine into folk systems of healing, ayahuasca has remained an important element in folk healing practices. Healers use the visionary vine to determine the magical cause of illness, and to neutralize or deflect the evil their clients believe responsible for their sickness.

# Iquitos:
# An Ethnography

## Iquitos—Its History

Despite the modern facade of the city of Iquitos, traditional jungle life with roots in a not so distant primitive past has by no means disappeared or even given ground before the impact of coastal industrialization. Although the casual visitor cannot help but note just how much of twentieth-century machinery and ways have entered into jungle life (at least as far as the existence of motor-powered launches, automobiles, airplanes, telephones, movies, pumps and odd-job machinery goes), nonetheless he would find many traditional beliefs flourishing in this relatively modern urban setting. Magical beliefs flourish in this situation of culture change, as man attempts to achieve mastery and control over the unknown by special rituals and ceremonies. Real problems are presented to the anthropologist who tries to separate the myriad strands of imported industrial society found among a small sector of the population from the admixtures of beliefs held by the destitute poor or middle-income men and women who attribute illness and misfortune to witchcraft.

Iquitos is a relatively new city. Penetration of the jungle region by the Peruvian national state was not easy because of the inaccessibility of vast tracts of land lying to the east of the high Andean mountains. However, the jungle was explored during the sixteenth century, as Spanish conquistadores heard tales of the fabulous land of El Dorado, which they believed lay

49

toward the east. At the time of the Spanish conquest in 1541, the adventure-bound, fortune-seeking captains of Pizarro were driven by one shared ambition —the desire to gain wealth and govern a territory of their own. Several expeditions set out from the coast to find the fabulous land of El Dorado, but to no avail.

There was a persistent belief that this golden land was located in the Amazon region. One expedition in 1541, led by Gonzalo Pizarro (a brother of the Peruvian conqueror) and Francisco de Orellano, set out from the coast with a force of 340 Spanish soldiers (only half of whom had horses) and some 4000 armed Indians. They crossed the high Andes, experiencing great distress and many problems. Perhaps three-quarters of them died before their journey finished. Instead of the famed land of El Dorado, they found only a "green hell," heavy rains, tropical fevers, and scanty Indian populations whom they tortured in the hope of extracting secret information. Under such torture the Indians told the soldiers that the land they were seeking was further and further to the East. All in all, well over 2000 miles of unknown land was visited by the survivors of the expedition, who finally reached the Atlantic Ocean after many months of weary travel (Coriat, 1943: 190–191; Fuentes, 1908: 156).

Despite such explorations, a permanent political-administrative center was not established in the rain forest until the Department of Loreto was created in 1861, some eight years after the first steamship entered what is now Iquitos. Augustine, Jesuit, and Franciscan missionaries who brought dispersed Indian groups under control were among the few to penetrate into this region. Wars of Indian extermination followed. Until the mid-nineteenth century, the Amazonian plains were a relatively unpopulated area. The advent of the rubber boom in the latter part of the nineteenth century added to the decimation of Indian populations, while generating both a large European and local migration of people who flocked to the jungle to get rich quickly by extracting the black gold from the heart of the forest. Iquitos' growth was due directly to the boom, and the rural areas took on their present day character of isolated hamlets, separated from one another by enormous distances, because of the very nature of the rubber extractive techniques which developed out of working the rubber trees. A ratio of several hundred acres per person to work was often set up.[1] Although the Department of Loreto today covers some 37% of the total land area of Peru, it is still thinly populated with only 4% of the nation's population inhabiting the area.

---

[1]See the excellent study done by the National University of San Marcos (1964) which deals with the history of this region.

## Present Day Iquitos

A virtual island in the jungle, the Amazon port of Iquitos at the time of the study welcomed both local jungle produce from outlying hamlets as well as ocean liners steaming in from far distant ports, carrying products such as radios, television sets, phonographs, blenders, and other modern consumer goods. They are offered for sale in small shops on the main street and attract tourists from other areas of Peru. A national law made the Department of Loreto a tax-free area in order to help develop its economy, and middle-class vacationers shopped in Iquitos to save money on household purchases, imported fabrics, electronic equipment, and fancy tinned foods and wines from abroad.

Aside from the main street filled with small commercial enterprises lined up in rows in the steaming sun, there are two large plazas that attract in their respective fashions middle-class families and urban poor in the main downtown area. As one wanders throughout the rest of the sprawling city, paved streets give way to mud-packed thoroughfares. Less than 30% of the houses found in Iquitos are considered modern, inhabitable structures and only 6% are considered even standard in a government-sponsored survey (Wils, 1968: 55). Fine brick and cement dwellings clustered around the downtown area give way to poorly constructed wooden houses that often have palm roofs and outdoor privies (*Ibid.*: 124).

The city has an estimated population of 120,000, and three clear-cut social segments are easily discernible to the social scientist as well as elicited from interviews. Housing, dress, nutrition, and skin color mark these different groups of people. First in the floating slum of Belén and scattered around in many *barriadas* or squatter settlements that girdle the city, one finds the civilized Indian, called *Cholo*—dark skinned, nominally Roman Catholic, and gripped by a magical world view whose roots extend back to the jungle and primitive days in river edge horticultural communities. Living at the edge of starvation, this group stays alive as best it can by a series of makeshift occupations and in particular, wholesaling of jungle produce: women and children run small stands where cooked foods and fruit are available for sale at a low price; or else men and women work as artisans if they have learned skills through tedious apprenticeships. If they have their own boats and nets, they work as fishermen or join forces as a group to pool their meager resources. Wils found this group to represent roughly 40% of his sample, one-quarter of whom lived in Belén, where they constituted approximately 71% of the slum population (1968: 11.7).

Another major segment—one referred to as *trigueños*—is lighter in pigmentation and acutely aware of the nuances of skin hues and hair form which set

them apart from the hated *Cholo*. This group, constituting about 35% of Wils sample *(Ibid.)* includes artisans, clerical personnel and at times, itinerant peddlers, as well as noncommissioned army personnel and their families. As a group, they are more involved in Roman Catholic activities and treat the *Cholo* they meet in the marketplace, in domestic service, and the like with obvious and open disdain. Women are carefully protected and accounted for, which contrasts to the relative physical mobility found among the poor. Middle-class values of chastity and decorum contrast to the expectations of the poor.

Finally, there is a self-admitted "high-society," who greedily follow the host of local radio programs and news columns which highlight their socialite activities. This smaller group is composed of tradesmen and their families, high government officials, army officers and professionals—many of whom have migrated to the jungle from coastal and highland cities. Much better educated that the other two groups, and representing some 12% of the population, they tend to be lighter-skinned as a group, even given the vast array of Mestizo physical characteristics that one encounters in Peru *(Ibid.)*.

### The Cholification Process
### Among the Poor of Iquitos

Before we examine the world of the *Cholo* more closely in order to understand how ayahuasca healing is an expression of the beliefs, values, and expectations of the urban poor who comprise the major clientele, we ought first to think about the process whereby river-edge, horticultural men and women became caught up in the "civilization process."

Western influence has been felt throughout the northwest Amazon for over four centuries, as tribal Indian groups have had their traditional patterns of behavior interrupted by European penetration. Not so very long ago, the poor of Iquitos and those living along the many river inlets were Indians. As the process of Cholification took place, aboriginal patterns disappeared or were distorted, but were not replaced with meaningful national ones. Despite the forces of deculturation that were at work, with Choloized Indians losing many cultural traits from aboriginal society, such as hammock making, ceramics, and the like, writers today such as Lathrap (1970) maintain that we can find behind the remnants of such societies evidence for a great forest civilization in the past.

As the result of race mixture between European and Indian over the last few hundred years, one encounters in modern day Peru the Mestizo as the major social segment.

Yet, lurking somewhere in the realm of non-Indian and non-Mestizo, one can find this third group, the *Cholo*. In the Colonial Period, it was thought that the word itself was a derogatory term for dog (Varallanos, 1964: 5). Varyingly defined in other regions of Peru with highly developed Incaic traditions or in the coastal desert strip, the *Cholo* tends to represent a relatively well-to-do Indian, who seeks the status of Mestizo, but who has not yet arrived. The *Cholo* is in an ambiguous status: he is not an Indian in the eyes of the Indian, nor a Mestizo in the eyes of a Mestizo. In this dual refusal, the *Cholo* finds his identification (Larson and Bergman, 1969: 66). These authors see the *Cholo* not as a class nor as a cultural entity, but rather as members of a contingent elastic category in which a great variety of persons who occupy marginal settings between traditional Indian and Mestizo worlds are found. Probably what is most important is that although the *Cholo's* social origins are akin to those of the Indian, his income and occupational independence relate him more closely to the Mestizo.

Various writers have looked at the actual process of transformation in urban or rural areas from being a member of an Indian group to becoming a *Cholo* (see Fuenzalida, 1970). We have, however, little material available to us on this "cholification" process in the rain forest, despite an occasional monograph on an Indian community or a study of a Mestizo population. One of the main factors that marks the *Cholo* in the historical process of change from one social status to another is the great geographical and occupational mobility spurred on by military conscription. The *Cholo* is certainly differentiated from the Indian by his participation, however marginal, in the national culture and his identification and social consciousness (Larson, 1969: 141).

As mentioned in passing in chapter three, similarities in cultural traits in the tropical rain forest region are far greater than differences. Although linguistic diversity is widespread, cultural bilingualism has been an important factor in facilitating the trade and commerce supposed for this area in prehistoric times. Traditionally, the tropical rain forest has been marked off from the more developed Andean civilizations to its West by the absence of monumental architecture and metallurgical refinements (Lowie, 1949: 1). Nonetheless, syntheses of recent archaeological data by Lathrap (1970) have pointed up a relatively high level of technological development which was not previously conceded for this region. As horticulturalists using slash-and-burn methods, traditional Indian groups had highly developed pharmacopoiea of medicines and herbs which were known and used in curing, religion, witchcraft, and divination. Shamans were highly valued and greatly elaborated belief systems concerning the spirit world existed. These shamans, or medicine men, often operated as doctors whose job it was to detect sorcerers. Medicinal use included emetics, purgatives, vapor baths, and special diets.

Historical data during the conquest period and later elucidates how basic life patterns were altered and finally destroyed in most areas of the northwest

Amazon. From the early explorers to the Catholic missionaries, to the small-scale Mestizo traders who set up outposts in areas rich in pelts, tropical fish, or particular crops, to the effect of the rubber boom and the unscrupulous rubber barons who literally enslaved thousands of Indians in a debt-peonage system (see Varese, 1970: 8), traditional ways of behaving were not permitted to remain intact. The introduction of a money economy and the inroads of the military further hastened the process of change.

The *Cholo* emerges in the midst of these several hundred years of culture contact. Here, contact took longer to reach him than it did in the Peruvian coast or highlands. Until the advent of gasoline powered motors, journeys were longer and more hazardous than they are today. Now, small one-engine army planes serve to bring the most inaccessible hamlets into line, and the church and military are two major institutions which give structure to the thousands of scattered hamlets in the jungle where not so long ago Indians lived.

Since the Second World War, residents of far-flung jungle hamlets have migrated to large cities like Iquitos. Although in a biological sense, the *Cholo* in Belén today may be physically indistinguishable from many Mestizos in the city itself, his world is different from that of the city dweller. The city saps the strength and energy of the jungle farmer and trader, whose labor it is that makes the shopkeeper rich. These merchants send off cheaply purchased, sleek, feline pelts to opulent stores in Paris or New York. Again, the exporters of tropical fish, who provide work at a pittance for near-starving thousands, are destroying natural resources by indiscriminate elimination of all that can be grasped. Not only do life styles differ at the river's edge, floating slum of palm-roofed, rickety balsa-supported houses (which represent almost one-sixth of the city's population), but racial undertones sharpen the ugliness of the contrast between rich and poor, with the term *Cholo* used as an insult against impoverished, dark-skinned man or woman.

The jungle abounds, nurtures, is full of danger. Yet, after long years of national control over an inaccessible jungle which only became effectively linked to the centralized coastal center by air routes during this century, Indian patterns of belief and cosmology reign, overlain with a somewhat tepid Catholicism.

Despite the relative richness of the frequently innundated jungle soil, health problems, such as those posed by parasitic microorganisms, make life difficult but not impossible for the river peasant. If only the peasant had a system of sewage and of water purification; if only he wore shoes to avoid the dangers of hookworm infection (that debilitating disease so widespread in the region[2]); if only he had cheap access to chemicals to kill the ants that voraciously devour

---

[2]Dr. Cornejo D. of the Faculty of Tropical Medicine, National University of San Marcos has pointed up the high level of hookworm infection rampant throughout the rain forest region (personal communication).

everything in sight—crops, houses, humans; if only he had transportation at a reasonable cost to bring his produce to market centers; if only there were schools that taught his children something of value, instead of pushing them sleepily out of a world of illiteracy into one of stumbling confusion. But the small farmer lacks most of the things that are necessary to make his jungle viable. He exists, he vegetates, he reconfirms the prejudices of the middle-class Peruvian, who meanders through the rivers in motor-launch, exploiting the poor farmer by selling staples that are not produced locally, since pelts or tropical fish earn more money in the short run. The *regaton,* as he is called, drinks beer and smokes fine cigarettes, not the simple *mapacho* tobacco produced in the region. He pays with the money he earns selling sugar, flour, salt, and other staples at exorbitant prices. The image of the jungle peasant, resting in his hammock, happy only when his belly is full of aguardiente is not a stereotype to be ignored. Like most such stereotypes, it often houses a grain of truth. To the peasant, the jungle is fearsome indeed, as poisonous snakes, small felines, constrictors, and a rich lore of spirits people his forest and pose a constant danger for him.

## Exploitation of the Poor

The jungle peasant has not been very successful in his rain forest niche, even during the rubber boom, when he was unwillingly entangled in a pernicious debt-peonage system. In this century, as the national society has spread its influence, unfulfilled promises of work have lured masses of migrants out of the jungle to the sprawling cities of Iquitos and Pucallpa. Over 43% of the population of Belén, for example, originated from nearby rain forest hamlets or other jungle areas (Oviedo, 1964: 116). When asked in sociological surveys why they left their jungle homes, they replied that schools for their children were lacking, or that they could barely stay alive on the few acres they possessed and hoped to find work in the city (*Ibid.:* 117). In fact, only 27% of the families in Belén own some land outside of the slum, while the overwhelming majority are completely landless. Poverty in Belén is further visible in terms of the simple lack of basic necessities for urban living. More than 73% of the population lacks canoes (necessary for transportation when the slum is inundated part of the year), kerosene stoves, electricity, sewage, or drinkable water in their homes. More than half lacked radios or sewing machines, while over 70% of the community had no savings whatsoever (Grajeda, 1964: 15).

The simple changeover from a rural to an urban setting, however, did not prepare the jungle farmer very effectively for urban life, where a creole bias imported from the coast was inherently racist and very class-conscious. The jungle migrant to a large city like Iquitos was most often darkly tanned by the sun as well as being heavily pigmented. He met with an iron-like wall of hostility, as class lines crystallized around obvious markers of identification such as skin color. The poor *Cholo*—desperately seeking to better his lot in the city—nourished the dream of a little patch of land, his own house, and perhaps a small yard to raise animals. He rushed headlong into the city where he was traumatized by the reception he received, encountering a system that kept him at arm's length. He found little if any work waiting for him. The jungle's raw materials were there, but only to be exploited cheaply by the industrializing coast and foreign enterprises controlling the national economy.[3] His women were exploited sexually if they were to keep jobs as shopgirls, and malnutrition and poor schools for his children were the rule. The only difference now was that he lived crowded together with other poor farmers who like himself came from jungle hamlets traveling days and months by river to reach the city. Now he lacked adequate sewage or potable water, and epidemics of measles, whooping cough, and illnesses such as diarrhea and tuberculosis caused his children to die in droves. Chronic illness multiplied. Poor diet and fecal-infected river inlets were his source of water in an uncaring city and brought his children and himself debilitating hookworm, a parasite that lives in filth and consumes red blood cells. Even the middle-class entrepreneur or salaried government employee, living in a cemented city, suffers from this ailment. But he wears protective leather shoes and not the plastic sandal of the poor, used more as occasional adornment rather than to control the insidious parasites that enter the body through the foot and lodge themselves in the small intestines. They lower the body's hemoglobin until weakness, apathy and lack of energy grip the sick man, woman or child afflicted, whose body often remains underdeveloped because of the parasite's work.

High up in the city, among families possessing a fine, protein-rich, store-bought diet, which contrasts with the peasant's banana or rice staple, parasitosis is a controllable evil. Expensive drugstore medicines which are taken at given intervals conserve the strength of the affluent city dweller. Tinned meats from Argentina arrive in ocean-going boats from England, while New Zealand butter is preserved in frozen food counters in modern supermarkets. The peasant down below in the floating slum is a fisherman, but he must sell his catch in the Belén market, since these precious pennies enable him to buy a stalk of bananas to nourish his large and often sickly family. Meat is expensive and found at the table of the poor only on rare occasions. Forest game is plentiful, but avaricious hunters in the search of feline pelts ignore other small mammals in the jungle, as they must carry these precious skins long distances to city ports to be exchanged for a cash pittance.

---

[3]Matos Mar (1968) has edited a series of essays that point up quite clearly the extent of the foreign economic domination.

Iquitos then presents us with a contrast of rich and poor—including a large middle ground which must be shaded in with low-salaried employees, government workers, small shopkeepers, artisans, day laborers and skilled workers. Their houses range from the classic wooden jungle hut with thatched roof to the more finely built dwellings of cement and even brick. This middle group occupies an ambiguous position in this twentieth century city. Living on the fringe of a pre-industrial but nonetheless capitalistic society, their livelihood and aspirations are directly tied in with the economic system. Yet, many of their beliefs and attitudes are indubitably linked to traditional jungle life, as Western-style education is poor, and reading habits not well developed. One city library with few volumes and a couple of ragged bookstores bring the national culture to its doors; women, when they read, spend time looking at beauty magazines or comic-book type serialized novels. Aside from a new urban university with an inadequate library and staff, Iquitos remains shackled to tropical torpor and outside many of the cross-currents of the modern world.

### The Structure of a Slum

The urban slum of Belén appears to some tourists as a delightful mimicry of Italy's Venice, of Brazil's Manaus, or of a dozen or so charming spots around the world that provide aesthetic delight. Picturesque sunsets are silhouetted against quaint palm roofs, balsa supports, and flowing rivers. To the soldier on leave, Belén appears as a comfortable niche were available women may be had for a promise. To the merchant in the city above, Belén appears as a repository for cheap laborers, potential buyers for inexpensive merchandise, or customers for overpriced staples. To the policeman, Belén is but an irksome part of the beat, full of petty fighting, wife-beating, small-scale robberies, and the like. To the government employee, busy at work, piling up study after study of economic, nutritive or public health problems among the poor, Belén is a sad example of the much to be done in the improbable future. The Peruvian journalist, Rumrrill, has written that "Belén is a community castigated by misery, the promises of politicians and voracious fires." Kerosene, used as the main source of fuel, is placed in cans that once contained foodstuffs. Reworked and fitted with a wick to provide light, these makeshift lamps constitute a grave fire hazard because of the widespread wood construction of houses and easily flammable thatch roofs (Oviedo, 1964: 160). Poverty in Belén is all pervading. Men try to stay alive, working as peons unloading balsa rafts or boats laden with jungle produce to be sold in the city market. Or, men and women work as *rematistas,* small-scale buyers and sellers, who haunt the shores of the Amazon or Itaya Rivers (depending upon the time of year and water level). They buy up quantities of fish or bananas, fruit or vegetables, to be sold again at a small profit. Over 30% of the occupations represented in Belén fall into this category (*Ibid.:* 135). Some with capital, called *regaton,* buy up large quantities of staples like rice, sugar, salt, etc. Equipped with motor-powered boats, they ply the rivers and many hamlets, selling at a huge profit to the needy and isolated goods which bring one-third less in the city. Others fish (some 4% according to Oviedo, 1964: 135), but with rising populations and indiscriminate fishing, resources in the immediate area of Iquitos have long since disappeared. Voyages take the fisherman further and further away in search of fish such as Corvina and Paiche on trips averaging fifteen days to a month or more.

Belén is full of commercially-minded men, women and children who traffic in whatever is available in the messy business of staying alive. Accumulating capital is difficult at best, and in hard times the day-to-day struggle consumes all the energies of the poor. Women work very hard caring for numerous children, manning a market stall or washing clothing in fecal-infested inlets, since the only fountain supplying drinking water to the slum is located more than a mile from major sectors of the community.

In many ways, Belén serves as a prime illustration of what Oscar Lewis has called the "Culture of Poverty".[4] Traits that Lewis described in Mexico and Puerto Rico as part of such an existence, like feelings of hopelessness, despair, and fatalism and the breakdown of the family, spring to life in Belén, not the Belén of tourists who look for progress in the occasional, well-built house of a merchant, but in the Belén of misery.

The structure of family life in Belén is directly related to the economic insecurity that is so widespread in the community. Marriages are fragile things indeed, and abandoned women and their children line up for charity doles in a local church once a week. Households run by women constitute over 20% of the community (Oviedo, 1964: 97). The figure would probably be higher, except for the lack of work centers which might attract the migration of men and boys looking for decent wages. Lima is far away, and transportation is costly.

Chastity does not receive lip service as a value before marriage as it does among middle-class Peruvians in the same city, and childhood is not at all a protected period. Girls set up their own common-law families relatively early, with over 34% of those families in Belén of this type (*Ibid.:* 104). Children work at odd jobs after school, like shining shoes, selling cooked food or ices in the street to help their families out with the few pennies they can earn. Young girls often assist their mothers at a market stall for long hours or take

---

[4]See Lewis (1966). I am using his term merely as a heuristic device in the following discussion, since his model deals in large part with qualitative aspects of slum life, and does not adequately get at basic causes for such behavior.

Approaching Pueblo Libre from Venecia.

care of younger members of the family. Parental supervision of children is minimal most of the year, and bands of youngsters roam the streets of the slum in the dry season when it is easy to get around on foot and canoe travel is not necessary.

A man's dream is that his children will support him in his old age and a sign of an astute man is one who can boast that his children give him a daily sum of money to help him get by. Yet, despite this, both maternal and paternal responsibility are fairly low. The exigencies of life are such that mothers are often pulled out of their home to work, leaving youngsters of ten and eleven to prepare meals for their younger brothers and sisters. Little girls of four and more act as child nurses, more or less caring for newborn babies while the mother is busy at work.

Education for such children is available, but hardly utilized to its full potential. In a sample of 1581 persons (excluding children under six years of age), Oviedo found that only 100 had completed secondary school or better. Over 18% were illiterate and another 66% had not completed primary grades. This is a rather large number of people who are either totally or functionally illiterate, especially in terms of the demands made upon adults by the national society, with its well-established tradition of literacy. Although children seem to be receiving a better education than their parents, a large segment of school age populations, or some 25%, was reported not in school (Oviedo, 1964: 127). This is important to keep in mind, especially in light of Oviedo's finding that

87 households out of 300, or some 29%, showed former marital unions (*Ibid.:* 108). When people become ill, very often step-parents are seen as the evil perpetrators of magic.

Civil marriage, the only legal form recognized by the Peruvian government, is infrequent, and church unions constitute a larger percentage for the Belén population. Nonetheless, at least one in three unions surveyed is common-law and the figure is probably higher. Because of money problems arising from lack of steady employment, a young couple will often move in with one of their parents if there is room at home until they can save enough money to build their own balsa hut or move up into one of the twenty or so slum settlements that surround the city. Although nuclear families constitute 56% of the community, extended families consisting of aggregates of relatives represent 30% of Oviedo's sample (p. 95). Over one-quarter of the dwellings in Belén are occupied by more than one family (*Ibid.:* 53).

Should a couple decide to separate, one of the spouses will leave and often will move back to live with his or her family. If money is available, a man will give his wife a monthly pension for his children's support, but all too frequently this depends upon whether or not the father is working. Although it is frowned upon, a woman on occasion may take the initiative and leave her husband if he drinks too much—not merely on payday but consistently—and fails to support her and her children. It is not at all unusual for a woman to start up a new union with another man and leave her children by a former marriage with parents or relatives. The motif of the evil step-mother or father is widespread, and rather than raising a child with a step-parent, all kinds of shifting about of children take place in the interest of family peace.

Tension fills the relationships between husbands and wives. Although it is possible that this may be a carry-over from traditional life patterns, when a person's primary loyalty was to his kinsmen and not necessarily to his spouse, precarious economic conditions, along with little if any government help in land reform and redistribution or scientific aid in farming, is more likely a primary cause. A frequent complaint that women make to their confidants is that when their husband was courting them, all kinds of promises were made. He would build them a strong, wooden house with a zinc roof, or he would care for their children born from another union. Instead, the theme of *la mala vida* reigns—the bad life that a spouse has brought—filled with tragedy, bad luck, frequent death of children, miserable living quarters, inadequate food, and little if any moral support.

A man's worst fear is that his wife will betray him, especially if he is one of the many who travel the rivers on fishing trips that last long periods of time. The fear of being cuckolded presents a heartfelt anguish to the jungle peasant, as it no doubt does in many other parts of the world. Unlike middle-class

Peruvian families who circumscribe the daily activities of their women and attempt to ensure their chastity, slum residents have not the affluence nor leisure to treat their women this way. In order to stay alive, women spend a good deal of time away from their homes and the binds of kinship ties, working at market stalls where easy flirtations are common enough.

If a man works at a distant plot of land, he must leave his wife in the city to work as best she can as a *rematista* in the urban market. When he returns to Belén after a prolonged absence, neighbors will rush secretly to him to tell him of his wife's infidelity—of the other husband she had while he was gone. Envy and malicious gossip are all too common, and a woman speaking to a man on the street is cause enough to set tongues wagging furiously. When a husband is at home, he gets angry if he sees his wife talking to another man and prefers her to stay close by the house. Yet, despite some of the great difficulties in achieving marital harmony, this region of Peru is famous for its elaborate love magic.[5]

Before looking briefly at the host of charms, talismans, and rituals that men and women use in this area of the world to get and keep a mate, or else punish someone who has strayed, we might wish to consider for a moment why there should be such an immense series of activities tied in to love affairs and marriage. If relationships between the sexes were easy and confidence-inspiring, it might be logical to suppose that this would be unnecessary. Unfortunately, as we have just seen, this is not the case. Economic insecurity, which is rampant in the area, enters related spheres of life like social organization and, in particular, kinship and mating arrangements between people. A commonly heard remark in Belén is that when dawn comes, most people don't know where their next meal is to come from. Those pressures and irritations which are part of everyday life for a man faced with continual unemployment and no guaranteed or predictable source of income can only magnify with the normal demands of family life. In this culture of poverty which characterizes Belén, with its social disorganization, broken homes, abandoned children, and prostitution, it becomes obvious that two kinds of love are accepted by most people: one is clean and recognizable by spontaneous tender feelings between men and women which lead to a permanent relationship. This first kind of love, my informants tell me, never lasts. Rather, the second type of love, which results from witchcraft, is the only kind that endures.

Different types of love magic can be delineated for convenience's sake. The first type is benign, and consists of charms, orations, and potions that function in order to permit a man or woman to capture the affection of another. The women of Loreto are famous for their love charms, the well-known *pusanga* potions, which are slipped into a beverage and cause a man or woman to fall

---

[5]See Dobkin de Rios (1969a).

madly in love with the person who has prepared the charm. One young abandoned mother who lived in a two-storey balsa house and who depended upon her fisherman father and working mother for support, showed me a small bird called *tanrrilla,* which she kept as a household pet. This little bird was distinguished by its rather elongated, boney legs, which in the preparation of a charm are used as a hollow telescope. One merely has to view the beloved person through this telescope (from a distance and unseen by the beloved), avoid certain foods such as salt and lard for one day, and that person will become wildly enamored of whoever effects the charm. Should the beloved person, however, see who it is that is trying to bewitch him, the magic will be returned with increased potency. The bewitcher will become mad with love for whoever effects the charm.

Another example of benign magic is the use of a fragrant leaf called *congonillo.* Lydia, a mother of nine children, confided to me the secret of the success of her long marriage (not at all a usual occurrence in Belén). Although she was a practicing Roman Catholic and married in the church, she left nothing to chance, and when she married washed all of her husband's clothing in a concoction made from this leaf. She maintained that he could not leave her, even if he wanted to, as the charm that she cast in this manner was irrevocable, and Julio, her husband, hadn't the slightest possibility of departing. Lydia told me this story in front of her husband, and he didn't contradict her, nor smile at her presentation. People have great faith in the remedies they use to bring about stability in their marital relations.

Another plant of interest is called *shimi-pampana.* Small and odorless, this tuber is chewed into a fine mash by a woman who is desperately trying to catch a man. The mash is then mixed with a fine, store-bought perfume, which the girl puts on her body. In little time at all, the beloved is believed to be cured —that is, he is bewitched and falls madly in love with the perfumed enticer after he has been near her. The way in which such love charms have spread throughout Peru was brought home to me in a particularly poignant way when I visited Lima in the spring of 1969. A secretary to a large corporation official in Lima, with whom I came into contact, asked me to please bring her some *shimi-pampana* from Loreto the next time I could, as her niece was in love with a young engineer and was having little success with him. I sent the woman a small sample of the herb that one of my informants gave me and about two months later, on my next visit to Lima, was informed that the girl was about to be married. She had carefully chewed the tuberous root and mixed it with an expensive French perfume.

Malicious magic, more than any other, is believed to exist in the jungle. Under this heading we can include various attempts to cause harm to another person. Such magic is thought to provoke distress, illness, or bad fortune and is often practiced by someone who wants to get back a former lover or a common-law spouse who has taken up with another person. Envy of a man's love, of a happy home, or vengeance for a supposed wrong, rejection of a suiter, rivalry in love—all may contribute to a person's pursuit of evil magic. Aurora, a girl of twenty-one, lost weight and hemorrhaged because of the evil-wishing of a woman who maintained that Aurora was stealing her man. This nasty woman paid a witch some $86 to cause the girl's death. Aurora sought out the service of a spiritualist, who claimed to have captured the spirit of the witch. When the healer learned of the danger facing the girl, he was able to neutralize the evil magic and cure his patient.

Another case of interest is that of Josepha, who is living with a fisherman some thirty years her senior. Before he moved in with her, he lived for many years with another woman who Josefa now believes is responsible for whatever pain or illness she might contract, from a muscle strain to something more serious. She is steadily losing weight and is ready to break up her household for fear of the damage this woman may do her, even having spoken to her husband of her fears.

Many folk healers, including those who use ayahuasca, have their waiting room filled with abandoned women who want the healer to get hold of the spirit of the departed spouse to make him return. Many believe that they have been deserted because another woman, propelled by envy or vengeance, caused them magical harm. Malicious magic may take many forms, and people believe that a sudden pain is the key to realization that one has been bewitched. Such harm may take the form of a simple muscular ache to extremes of madness, unconsciousness, and possible death.

Another magic that can be related to the despair and desperation facing these poverty-striken people can be called preventative magic. In a place like Belén, laden with insecurity and inundated with poverty, a woman seemingly would have little choice but to be sure that the man she will go to live with is single and had had no other household tucked away somewhere else. Fearing the magical harm that may befall her if she lives with a man who already has another wife, many women consult folk healers called *curiosos*. For a small fee, they will consult a magic stone, fortune-telling cards or call upon spirits they control to be sure that the person in question has no other commitment. One girl, Maria, spoke of a romance that never materialized between herself and a young policeman. When she gave the man's name and address to one such folk healer, he went through a complicated ritual of investigation in which he rubbed a polished magical stone over her forehead and hands and told her to return three days later, when he informed her that the policeman had another woman. Maria, at twenty-two already an abandoned mother with one child, decided not to pursue the romance any further. One does not knowingly look for trouble by inviting vengeance manifest in the form of illness or bad fortune. Another woman who neglected to find out if her beloved had another woman became the victim of bewitchment, grew thinner and thinner, and was reputed to have died from this evil magic.

The last category of magic that can be delineated is called restitutive. A proliferation of folk healers exists, including those who cure with ayahuasca, and the *empíricos* whose task it is to heal illness caused by evil magic. Using techniques such as sucking out foreign objects from a woman's genital region placed there as part of magical harm *(daño),* or soothing an abandoned mother with a magical stone, or blowing cigarette smoke over a man whose woman has left him—these healers are kept quite busy. Many are called upon to get hold of the spirit of a deserted husband, and some boast of their powers to bring back such spouses from areas as far away as Lima.

These four categories of love magic give us some idea of the relationship between men and women in this jungle region. Because of the social disintegration that marks this culture of poverty, there is an elaborate series of beliefs and a cognitive system that set up certain expectations and values between men and women. The Hollywood ending, the capitalist ethos concerning love and its "forever after" commodity aspects has not touched this little pocket of city life in the Peruvian jungle. Needless to say, these capsulated tales of woe must be enlarged to include the daily brew of misery.

Thus, we see that magical beliefs about love are answers and attempts to deal with the ever-present social reality in which social disorganization is a distressing fact of life. Belief in the efficacy of these charms, talismans, and retributive devices are ways in which reassurance and some security and ease can be obtained by people who are never quite sure that they can count on a good tomorrow.

Magical beliefs in the Peruvian jungle are by no means limited to affairs of the heart, but rather are a general, persistent affirmation that people at bottom are cruel and envious, and can cause harm to others in the form of a generalized malice. Found among the poor and middle-income segments of the community, these beliefs in evil-wishing as well as the varied illnesses that *ayahuasqueros* are called upon to heal with the powerful potion of ayahuasca, will be examined in greater detail in the pages to follow.

# Ayahuasca
# Healing Sessions

Iquitos: The Search for a Healer

5

In Iquitos, when a poor person becomes ill and believes he is suffering from a disease caused by the malice of another, a visit to an ayahuasca healer may be suggested by a relative or friend. In Belén, Wils found that over 25% of the people he questioned preferred *empíricos* (folk healers) to doctors (1967: 131). My own impressions are that this is a conservative figure. Certainly, residents of Belén tend to seek assistance in times of crises rather than at the first sign of trouble or for preventative reasons.

The process of getting oneself healed may be a slow one if the sick person shops around for a healer who is reputed to have cured many people, who is wise in the use of the purge, and who knows which herbs will heal. Several people may be seen before the sick person settles upon a healer who can give some promise of being able to help him. The selection of a healer is matched by a similar sifting of patients, since the *ayahuasquero,* too, is careful to accept only those with whom he believes he may have some measure of success. A healer will refer patients to hospital or private medical facilities if he thinks the illness is a simple one which needs medication or X-rays. He will often reject patients who are psychotic—whose disease is in effect a total flight from reality and who consequently may not be reachable under the effects of the drug. The healer will also accept some patients to whom he will not administer ayahuasca. Their illness may have been chronic in na-

67

ture, leaving them weak after a period of long physical suffering. Vomiting and diarrhea, continually reported in the wake of the initial hallucinogenic experience, may be too much for such a person. In many cases, the healer himself will prescribe pharmaceutical medicines, which in most South American countries require no prescription and are available to anyone who can pay the price.

The process of referring patients to medical personnel in cases of simple organic disease has its counterpart in the frequent referrals of patients to the drug healers by medical doctors attached to the city hospital and in private practice. Formal psychiatric facilities in jungle cities are relatively rare[1], and university training in underdeveloped countries, as in the United States, generally prepares the doctor for a focus on organic rather than psychological illness. For these latter illnesses, the folk healer is probably better prepared, as his general expectations are that a patient will suffer from socially precipitated illnesses which have resulted from stress, conflicts, tensions and the like. To the healer, interpersonal referents are as important, if not more so, than organic symptoms.

Rarely does a sick person go to a healing session by himself. The drug's effects are such that someone often must see him home afterwards. Weakness and debility generally follow the three of four hours of strong dizziness produced by the drink. Moreover, the presence of a loved one such as a spouse, parent, or brother may be necessary to reassure the patient when his visions fill with frightening and fearsome jungle beasts or monsters of his own imagination. Interestingly enough, feelings of camaraderie are often generated during the course of a drug session, even among men and women who may not be known to one another. On some occasions, however, groups of individuals may be attending several sessions together, if their illness requires several weeks or longer to heal. But generally, groups of total strangers sit around in a circle, taking ayahuasca along with the *maestro,* as he is called. If one were to visit such a group merely to observe, it would be difficult to know those present were strangers, since people seem to care so much about one another. By the time the full effects of the drug are experienced by participants, and especially if the experience is a good one with a well-prepared potion, the warmth, concern, friendship, and care radiating within the group stand out as an obvious characteristic of the session.

---

[1]In fact, in Peru as Seguín points out (1970: 175), there are about 100 psychiatrists in practice, 90 of them in Lima, the capital. Of the total of 2010 psychiatric beds in the nation, 95% are in Lima. The rest of the country, which has 83.4% of the population of Peru, has only 93 psychiatric beds.

### The Healing Sessions

Most drug healing in Iquitos today takes place in a jungle setting on the outskirts of the city. Several evenings a week, a healer and his assistants or wife assemble a group of patients ranging from three or four in number to larger groups of twenty or thirty. About six or seven o'clock at night, a healer may leave his home with his bottled preparation in a small sack, along with his *schacapa,* a rattle made from tying together a bunch of dried leaves that is used to accompany songs and whistling. He will collect some of his patients as he goes toward the place that has been decided upon for the session. Many times, patients will meet at the healer's home, as he may be busy there curing people during late afternoons. All of them may go by bus to the farthest point on the line, and then walk for an hour or two to their destination. Other times, they may take a motor-powered canoe or they may paddle for a few hours to some secluded place. Such settings are chosen because people who take ayahuasca, as with other hallucinogens, can be hypersensitive to sound. The frequent motorcycles that roam through the city can be disturbing to a patient if a session is held in a houseyard near a noisy city street.

As the city has grown, the jungle has receded further and further away, making transportation to it difficult. Today almost no virgin jungle is found less than half an hour away by motor boat. Healers say that the jungle is a better place to "work" not only because there is less noise, but also because the songs the *ayahuasquero* sings are penetrating and there is sometimes the fear that he may be reported to the police if overheard. Some city doctors are jealous of the success of their ayahuasca rivals and are reputed to be quick to make formal complaints. Interestingly enough, it is not against Peruvian law to take natural substances like ayahuasca to alter states of consciousness. It is against the law, however, to practice medicine without a license. City noises, too, can cause visions to disappear quickly, or become distorted, which could cause the patient to have a bad trip, especially in those cases where additional psychedelics such as *Datura suaveolens* may make the drug experience difficult for the patient under the best of circumstances. Should time be lacking to reach a forest clearing, a closed balsa house in Belén can serve as the place where healing takes place. If it rains, a wall-less shelter in the open forest with a thatched roof, called a *tambo,* may be used.

Patients bring small gifts of *mapacho* cigarettes or perfumed water to the session. These gifts may be used by healer and patient alike. If love incantations are to be performed, a client may bring something with him which belongs to his beloved. Many carry plastic drop cloths to sit on since the jungle floor is damp and sessions may last until three or four in the morning. As the healer and his patients arrive at the chosen spot, a light banter often is heard. People

An ayahuasca healing session in a jungle clearing.

settle down around a circle, something which many healers believe is necessary precaution to keep the evil spirits of the jungle or those sent by other jealous healers or witches at bay. At about 10 P.M., the healer will take out a communal cup in which the ayahuasca drink will be distributed. Reciting an oration and whistling a special spell as protection for each person who drinks, the healer passes the cup around the circle. The amount of the potion will be varied in accordance with many factors, including what the healer assessed the body weight and physical strength of the person taking the purge to be. This will be one determinant of whether a patient receives a little or a lot. Is it the first or seventh time the person has had ayahuasca? From what illness is he suffering? The optimal dose found by Rios Reategui seems to be 7 mgm. per kilogram of body weight.[2] My impression from the various sessions I attended is that the healer will give a larger dosage to a person whose complaint is psychosomatic—illness with physical symptomatology but whose origin is believed by both to be due to some kind of magical harm. More about psychosomatic illness in Chapter Six.

Typically, the last one to drink is the healer. Some, in fact, prefer that no patient follow after him, so that those present can reach a climax in their visions as close together as possible. Needless to say, this enables the healer to be most effective in communicating with all his patients simultaneously. As long as half an hour may be necessary for the effects of ayahuasca to be felt, although reaching the height of visions may take longer for some individuals. People will sit around smoking and chatting. At times, someone may get up to vomit or defecate off to the side. The sounds made are not hidden from those present, and the healer may use the opportunity to talk to the rest of the group about what is happening. He may stress how effective the purge is and how important it is that each person try to keep it down in their stomachs for a long as possible, so that their visions will be both good and strong. If a patient has had no effects from the drug (which does happen on occasion), another portion may be meted out by the healer. Rarely, it may take as many as six or seven consecutive drinks until someone's visions begin.

In these instances, the fault may be with the healer, especially if he does not have his own fields to cultivate the vine. Thus, he may have to pay others to bring him ayahuasca for preparation and he may not be sure about the potency of the various ayahuasca species that are available in the region. The plant he receives may be dried out, or too small a quantity for everyone who plans to take a share.

With the growth of the city in recent years, it has become more and more difficult to obtain the quantity of ayahuasca that was formerly possible. The price of the vine has risen, and although some healers try to maintain their own

---

[2]Rios Reategui (1962)

psychedelic gardens, others must make frequent trips back and forth from their farms in order to bring the materials back to the city. Others pay people to travel to outlying hamlets for the liana, and such healers must have cash on hand to pay for their cuttings. Ayahuasca in the vicinity of Iquitos has long since been drunk up.

Healers use a good deal of Quechua (the highland language of the Andean region) in their songs during the ceremony. Whistling, too, often is part of the session and is interspersed throughout the evening's activities. As the hours pass, the healer moves around the circle contacting each person in turn, accompanied by his ever-present *schacapa* rattle which gives forth a rustling, rattling noise. During the curing ceremony, the healer will blow *mapacho* cigarette smoke over the body of a sick person, and if his patient is suffering pain in a particular part of his body, the healer will suck the dolorous area, often bringing forth a spine or thistle which those present believe was magically introduced by an enemy or evil spirit. Throughout the session, each patient receives counseling and is ritually exorcised by the healer.

Finally, at two or three in the morning, after some four or five hours of strong drug intoxication, the patient either returns to his home, or elects to spend the night in a nearby *tambo*. Dietary prescriptions are an integral part of ayahuasca healing because of a belief that the vine possesses a jealous guardian spirit. To propitiate this spirit, patients refrain from eating salt, lard, or sweets for at least twenty-four hours preceding and following the use of the purge. In addition, special diets may be prescribed by healers for particular patients, or sexual abstinence prior to a session may be demanded.

## Description of a Session

One interesting session took place near the edge of the city, close by one of the small river inlets leading to the Amazon. Don Luis, the healer, four of his patients, two assistants, and I met at the healer's house in Venecia. We walked several miles past open countryside to a clearing where we spread our plastic mats on the ground in a circle. Luis, whom I had met in Belén, was born in a small hamlet a few hours by boat from Iquitos. The fifth son of a small farmer, he left home when he was eighteen to serve in the army. Sent to a distant outpost near the Colombian border for two years, he eventually decided to live in Iquitos, where he was apprenticed to a carpenter. A distant uncle of his was an *ayahuasquero* and through his influence, Luis became interested in healing with the plant. For several years he worked with his relative, learning the ayahuasca songs and taking the potion at frequent intervals to assist his uncle in treating patients. Each August, he and his teacher would go by boat to an uninhabited part of the rain forest, where they would literally renew themselves and learn from the drug, as well as to strengthen themselves against the dangerous envy of witches. Such malice was thought to be an ever present threat to their healing successes. In these retreats, Luis experimented with various combinations of drug plants which his uncle taught him to prepare. He also spoke at great length with his teacher about the patients he had treated, their symptoms, and the remedies he prepared for them.

One day, while under the effects of ayahuasca, Luis had a vision which indicated to him that he was now ready to take patients on his own. Although he still practiced his trade of carpentry in Iquitos, he spent many hours receiving and treating patients, both at home and in drug sessions that he usually held two or three times a week, depending on the number of patients he thought should take the drug. After I was introduced to Luis and visited him several times in his home, watching him treat patients who came for counseling and exorcism of evil spirits, I was invited to attend an ayahuasca session. Twice the session had to be postponed because rain was imminent, apparently something which happened with regularity to healing sessions in Iquitos. That Tuesday night, however, the skies seemed reasonably clear and we reached our destination some three of four miles outside of Iquitos with little difficulty. I walked alongside two young women, one of whom was a patient. Her sister was there to see her home later that night. When we spread our mats in a circle, the atmosphere was informal. Several people smoked cigarettes throughout the session.

Luis whistled some special incantations over the cup he used to distribute the potion and in turn handed it to each man and woman. As usual, although the rest of the group were unknown to one another, they wished the person taking the purge good health as it was drunk. The amount of the drink was varied by the maestro for each person, and he was the last to drink. Some twenty-five minutes passed while Luis waited for the effects of ayahuasca to be felt. Chatting with each person in turn, he walked around the circle to talk to patients and to ask them if they were feeling any dizziness. He continued to whistle and moved his foot steadily to keep pace with the music. At times, he shook his *schacapa*. At this point in the session, after an hour or so of observing and listening, I felt a state of ease and tranquility even though I had not taken ayahuasca. The quality of the singing was quite soothing in its effects. As in many sessions I attended that year, several people were afflicted with heavy vomiting, a common side effect of the potion, although they didn't seem visibly upset by this. The healer continued whistling and singing, occasionally counseling patients and remarking, "*Joven* (young man), you've had this sickness a long time, I will cure you," etc.

My sense of well-being lasted for about an hour and a half until it began to rain. Then we took shelter under a nearby *tambo*. By the time we were

resettled under the shelter, most of the people who had taken ayahuasca that night were at the height of their visions. The general mood of the group was easygoing and friendly, which contrasted enormously to the formal treatment one person accorded another at the beginning of the evening, when strangers who were known only to the healer met for the first time.

At this point, one man began to cry and said to no one in particular that his chest was full of tears. Another man patted his back to console him, advising him not to cry for any woman. During this period which lasted for about an hour, the healer counseled each patient openly in front of the rest. One older woman, doña Manuela, complained that she felt she was dying. Don Luis listened to her, but did not reply. This feeling of death and rebirth occurs frequently in sessions and is related no doubt to the feelings of loss of self at the height of entering an altered state of consciousness (see Ludwig, 1969: 16).

The healer went on to speak to me about an older man who was at the session but who was not taking ayahuasca. This patient, he said, had cancer and was told at the city hospital that they could do nothing for him. Nonetheless, Luis was certain he would be able to cure him by means of a special diet which he was prescribing. He spoke about another patient who had suffered the same illness and was now cured. The healer was full of boasts about the people he had helped. At the same time, he deprecated the performance of other healers who he said were jealous of his success and who did not know how to heal. "They only know how to whistle and suck at affected parts of the body," he said. Although Luis did not use the latter technique in healing, it is found quite commonly among all types of regional healers; a patient for example, who might have a pain in a particular part of the body would stretch out so the healer could such at the effected area, often removing a thorn or worm which he would claim he extracted from the painful area. I observed this procedure several times during both ayahuasca and non-ayahuasca sessions and was on occasion permitted to examine the slimy creature that was extracted from the healer's mouth before he spit it out with vehemence. Many among the urban poor maintain the traditional Indian belief that such thorns and worms are sent to their patient as part of magical harm—introduced into their body by a malign spirit to cause illness. The only radical cure for such an illness is to suck out this *chonta*. That a healer might introduce a foreign object into his mouth secretly before beginning the sucking procedure doesn't seem to occur to many patients.

At this particular session, Luis had two assistants with him. A woman, the doña Manuela mentioned earlier, once had her child cured by Luis a long time ago. She often returns to drink ayahuasca and to sing the healing songs along with him. Another man, Eduardo, who also felt gratitude toward Luis for curing a relative, frequently worked with him. In the past, he had been apprenticed to another healer, but claimed that his original teacher was jealous of his visions. That man's envy inhibited Eduardo's ayahuasca visions, so that he felt he had no choice but to terminate his training. He is now working with Luis, whom he believes to be a morally superior person and more effective curer.

The session ended about 2 A.M., and the patients began their long walk home. I accompanied the two girls to their home, but found the ayahuasca patient very uncommunicative about her experience. She never came to Luis' session again. Many of the other patients had to cover distances of five or six miles, although a few who felt weakened by the purge slept at the *tambo*. At dawn, when they felt stronger, they made the journey back.

# Witchcraft and Illness

When the Spanish came to America at the end of the sixteenth century, they were in many ways typical representatives of the Middle Ages—a time in which illnesses were viewed by these exceedingly devout Catholics as God-given. Mental illness was seen to be supernaturally caused by means of demon possessions and exorcism was a well-known ritual within the church.

The few doctors who accompanied the Spanish adventurers to Peru were probably not well-trained, experienced men of medieval universities, but rather, as Lastres (1951) points out, vagabonds and adventurers who went from town to town, peddling their remedies in order to make a living. By 1538, there was talk in Lima of charlatans, curing with *ensalmos*—magical orations and "superstitions" which they brought with them from Spain (*Ibid.:* 25).

In 1541 when the first expedition of Pizzaro set out to the Amazon region, it is likely that a trained medical person, called *cirjuano* (surgeon), accompanied the group on its journey. There is in fact some speculation that ayahuasca was first taken by Europeans as a result of this expedition (Lastres, 1956: 115). For the most part, however, such trained medical personnel and clerics as well were zealous in their religious beliefs and considered most if not all indigenous medicine as absurd and the work of the devil. In actual fact, the New World had a rich herbatorium of plants used in native healing which had no counterpart in Europe. Although the Spanish in their political domination of Peru attempted to control native systems of medicine, many indigenous beliefs concerning illness remained fairly intact, in some cases only to become mixed with those of Spanish vagabonds in their fortune-seeking adventures.

Spanish control of the rain forest was less secure than control of either the coast or highlands because of geographic factors mentioned earlier. The jungle's indigenous beliefs concerning causality of illness persisted with the least amount of change, when compared to other regions.

## The Etiology of Illness

As in many parts of the world where beliefs in magic, withcraft, and sorcery are handmaidens to modern medicine, one finds that people seek different sets of answers to the eternal problems of illness. How one's body has been attacked by micro-organisms and how illness spreads throughout it are not questions of much interest in a world where causal factors are viewed primarily within a magical framework. Thus, "why me?" and not "how?" is the subject of inquiry into disease and all its ramifications. A person's concern upon entering a period of impaired or lessened functioning in this part of the world, where drug healing is a flourishing fact of life, is to find out exactly why he, and not someone else, is afflicted by disease. Nor are the answers simple ones, especially in light of ongoing culture change where twentieth century medical science has made certain inroads.

As both the jungle peasant and urban poor see it, illness comes about in three distinct ways. First of all, simple complaints like colds, sore throats, skin infections, and the like are "God-given"; store-bought medicines, antibiotics, injections that are preferably painful (so as to ensure healing), and hospital treatment are chosen to heal such minor problems. Formal medical consultations are generally far too costly for poor people, and the city hospital has the reputation of a place that the poor go to in order to die. As a result, many badly trained medical technicians called *sanitarios,* who get their knowledge from purchased books, diagnose these uncomplicated ailments and prescribe medicines they think may be effective. Sometimes these technicians are of help, but it is doubtful if they maintain any standard of hygiene or have any real understanding of what they are doing. Should a person become worse after being treated by such an untrained person, it is believed that his illness does not fit into this category of simple affliction. Rather, the very fact that the patient's physical condition has worsened makes it an obvious fact to the jungle resident that the sick man or woman has been bewitched. Within this second category of magical illness, recognized by the suddenness of the onset of pains and aches attacking a particular part of the body, two finer divisions are made. Either the evil of people or else river and jungle spirits are responsible. No doubt these latter beliefs about the jungle as a place peopled with animistic beings date back to Indian times. Most trees, plants, and rivers have mother spirits which are viewed as jealous guardians of nature. For example the *Yacumama* or mother spirit of the river takes revenge upon any menstruating woman who paddles across in a canoe. A playful dolphin may be sent to overturn her boat, and only a clove of garlic worn on her body is a woman's protection in keeping the dolphin away. Should such an individual bathe before three days after her menstrual period have passed, it is believed that a river animal will be inserted in her vagina and cause her to hemorrhage. If she dares to walk through the forest while she is "unclean," the spirit of a lofty tree or the mother spirit of the forest may cause her a sudden pain, muscle ache or accident.

### Jungle Lore[1]

At twilight, when the light dims and the open hut of the peasant fills with the mystery of the jungle, birds begin to chant their frightening, high-pitched songs, sending chills down the spine of any who listen. These shrill penetrating whistles are believed to come from the *Tunchis,* the spirits of the recent dead who roam the earth. They live a limbo-like existence for an indeterminate time before they achieve any kind of final repose. They are believed to cause sickness, harming children and adults alike. When a person dies, a house may be abandoned for a week or so to allow the spirit of the dead person, who is believed to be retracing his steps on earth, to leave the site so that once again it will be fit for human habitation (Coriat, 1944: 83). As night falls throughout the jungle, many mothers will carefully exhale *mapacho* cigarette smoke over themselves and their children to keep these dangerous spirits at bay.

The forest, too, is full of danger for the person who wanders through it alone. Without warning, a creature with one spindly leg and the other over-sized, called *Chullachaqui* (unequal feet, in Quechua) may appear in the guise of a friend or parent. He is known to abduct little children and adults under the pretence of going to visit the home of a loved one. If the body is never found, the family knows that the missing person has been stolen, (Tovar, 1966: 83).

The river as well as the jungle is a fearful place. Belief in the *Yacuruna,* or spirit of the river, who can assume the disguise of a Christian man or woman to effect evil, is widespread throughout the region. He is pictured as a superior, amphibious being who carries his victims to the bottom of the river and

---

[1]Although the folklore accounts in this part have been published (see the various citations in this section), the tales recounted here have been elicited from informants during the course of fieldwork. Variations do occur from one person to another, but many motifs remain the same.

Yando '71

converts them into one of his own. There is an immense city below the rippling, mostly muddy river waters which is populated by strange creatures. This city is a reverse image of those found on land, completely upside-down, with the creatures that inhabit it having their heads on backwards. Living in palaces of crystal, with walls of multicolored scales and pearl, the *Yacuruna* is sovereign among 2000 different species of fish that populate the fertile Amazon. His seat is that of a turtle, and his feet are protected by sandals made of their shell. At night, he sleeps in a small, high shelter resting on a net made of gazelle feathers, with one eye closed and the other watching out for ferocious crocodiles. His sleep is protected by a mosquito net made of the flowered, silky wings of butterflies, woven together by lightening bugs. Immensely powerful, he can change his shape at will, ascending to the highest clouds to cause storms of torrential dimension. Tearing up treetrunks with his muscular arms, he presents a constant danger to the river navagator. He is responsible, too, for the fearful *mal pasos,* those horrific whirlpools which made heavily laden canoes and small boats overturn (Ramirez, 1963: 72).

Serving the *Yacuruna* is a legion of river dolphins.[2] These much-feared mammals populate jungle waters and are thought to couple with human beings. Possessed of magical powers, they, too, can change into a human being, a well-dressed Christian who goes to parties and dances just like anyone else. The dolphin generally lures his victim to the water's edge and carries him off. Although the land under the water is frightening to consider, it is portrayed in popular accounts as a magnificent, splendid city which draws visitors to permanent residence, much to the regret of their loved ones who are left behind on land. This underwater city is a paradise when compared to its earthly counterpart (Herrera, 1965: 48).

Fishermen who manage to overcome their fear of the dolphin will kill it to make a love charm from its female genital organ. Those suffering from unrequited love carefully dry the skinfold of this organ, which they then hide on their arm or in the palm of their hand, being careful to abstain from salt and lard for one day. When they meet the person they love, they may shake hands or give the casual Peruvian *abrazo* (a sort of arm around the shoulder touch), all the while being sure that the hidden charm touches the beloved person. The belief is that within no time at all the woman will fall madly in love with the bewitcher. However, should he forget to observe the food taboos, the charm will boomerang, and he will become even more wildly enamoured of the person he loves.

Water sirens are other creatures both admired and feared by the jungle farmer. When out fishing alone, he may see a lovely, light-skinned girl, who

---

[2]The sweet water dolphin is very common near Iquitos and much feared for its alleged magical powers. Pinedo (1966) has identified it as *Delphinis fulviatis.*

is half-fish and half human, appear before him. Sirens are reputed to cause the disappearance of men by enticing them with their songs and carrying them off to the land below the water. No doubt belief in the siren dates from European contact during the rubber epoch.

## Modern Medicine and the Urban Poor

Given the nature of economic and social exploitation of the poor and the miserable educational facilities which are generally too expensive for most parents to utilize for their children (who can better serve them economically at odd jobs), it is no wonder that animistic beliefs from the traditional past remain so firmly entrenched in twentieth-century life, despite the presence in Iquitos of Euro-American medicine. The quality of medicinal treatment, when available, is not very good, and relations between Euro-American medical personnel and the poor are very bad indeed. These medical personnel are generally drawn from upper segments of the national society and share the prejudices against and distaste for the inferior *Cholo*. Without doubt, this reinforces the mutual stereotypes held by both. The paternal air of the nurse or doctor, the indifferent service received and the disinterest when money is unavailable on the one hand, do nothing to overcome the fear and rationalization that a hospital and the doctor's medicine are good only for simple ailments. The destitute poor who live in Belén find the ayahuasca healer far more effective than the indifferent medical services available to them. As we will see shortly, drug healers not only use store-bought medicines, but prepare special tonics, herb baths, and diets for their patients, as well as utilizing an immense number of plants and vegetable substances in their treatments. Their psychological assurance and warm manner of treating patients contrasts enormously to the disdainful disinterest that characterizes most interpersonal contacts between the medical doctor and the poor patient. While the *ayahuasquero* gears his prices to the ability of his patient to pay, the large city hospital's public wards provide no medical service inexpensive enough for the empty pockets of the poor. When women go to the hospital to have their babies, they say they are badly treated by the doctors and nurses. Some women in fact, report having their babies on the floor and not on delivery tables. Medical services are poorly understood by the people of Belén. For example, informants would often discuss the required blood tests necessary by civil ordinance in order to obtain a job as a domestic or sales clerk. "My blood is bad" or "My blood is good" would be the response to inquiries on my part about the test, yet the nature of the serology performed or the purpose of the test was never clear in their minds.

Class barriers made communication between medical personnel and the destitute poor perfunctory, with condescension and disdain marking most encounters. For example, one family in Belén was caring for a distant relative, a young boy named David. He suffered from the common complaint of vomiting and diarrhea, which did not improve. During his mother's absence, the boy's cousin brought him to the city hospital for treatment one Friday. When the boy's relative returned the following Monday, they learned the child had died and had been promptly buried without anyone bothering to notify the next of kin, although their address had been recorded by hospital personnel. These heartless, disinterested encounters leave Belén residents with little respect for or faith in the medical personnel with whom they come into contact.

Death, too, presents the poor of Iquitos with a terrible dilemma. Unless a city doctor is in attendance upon a dying person (charging a fee that for most poor people represents a three to four day food budget), an autopsy as required by law must be performed before a permit for burial can be obtained. Since the autopsy, too, is costly, most residents of Belén bury their dead in a pauper's grave in a cemetery called San Juan, which is set on a beautiful plain of white sand and tropical flowers. Generally, no priest is in attendance and both young and old are laid to rest together.

## Magical Illnesses

Of the many complaints of illness that I listened to in Belén (except for those by men and women who had recently migrated to the city), most did not fit under the heading of evil brought by river or jungle spirits. Instead, case after case of illness was attributed by the suffering person to evil caused by others. Either a witch had been paid to bring magical harm to someone in the form of illness or death, or sorcery was resorted to when some powerful plant might be slipped into a drink or thrown across a person's threshold in the still hours of the morning. It is from the many varied illnesses to be described shortly that much of the marginal population of the jungle suffers—ailments that may be summed up in large part under the term psychological or psychosomatic.

One such illness which afflicts both children and adults is a very special kind of fright called *susto*. A common illness found throughout Peru and Latin America, this infirmity includes many cases of profound alteration of metabolism or nervous disorders. It is one of the most frequent types of illness treated by Peruvian folk healers and originates from a violent impression of fear. Many believe that *susto* has supernatural origins in which the soul of a person has been magically separated from its body.[3] A sudden fall or loud noise may be the reason for a young child's continued crying, fretting, or sulky behavior over a long period of time. Symptoms include the child's withdrawal from normal,

---

[3]See Valdivia (1964) for his treatment of folk illness in Peru.

everyday activities. It is feared that babies will startle themselves by the sudden jerks of their arms and feet, and many mothers swaddle their newborn children for two or three months, wrapping cotton cloth around their body so as to limit their movements. Adults, too, are not exempt from *susto,* which in their case may come about from an unexpected incident in their lives. Two case histories illustrate this syndrome.

Danita, a little two-year old girl, was playing at the edge of her balsa house one day with no one in particular watching her. Her mother was in town, working as a seamstress; her father had long since run off to Lima, and her overworked grandmother was busy preparing the family meal. Arriving in Belén some eight years ago from Tamishiyacu, a distant jungle community, the grandmother had left her husband behind to work their fields of bananas and yucca. He sent her no money. Eight of her eleven children who were married barely had enough to keep themselves alive and could not help her out very much. This elderly woman's daily companion was constant anxiety. When her granddaughter, Danita, suddenly slipped off the edge of the balsa porch into the water, she would have drowned had the grandmother been a mere three steps further inside the one room shack. Fortunately, the child was pulled out. From that time on, however, over a period of three months, she was fretful and lost her appetite. In despair, the grandmother took the child to a spiritualist, who was curing her grown daughter of a disease they believed was sent by a jealous rival. Using incantations and spells, the spiritualist said he was able to capture the child's soul which had been lost when she fell into the river. This he duly returned to the little girl. Shortly after the evening session which I attended, when *mapacho* smoke was blown over the child's body, a noticeable change was evident in her behavior. She laughed and sang, danced to the transistor radio that played whenever there was money enough for batteries, and ate with her previous gusto. So successful was the treatment, that the healer used the child to boast of his curing abilities in front of potential clients, telling how "reasonable" his treatment was (it had cost the grandmother perhaps 15% of her monthly income).

A young woman suffering from *susto* did not have quite this happy ending to her tale of suffering. Separated from her common-law spouse, this woman in her early twenties took up with a young soldier and had a child. After a year and a half had passed, he left her to move back with his mother, who lived only a few streets away in Belén. The woman became excessively anxious about her nursing baby. Within a week, she reached a state of hysteria, stopped breast feeding the child, cried continually and began to talk to herself. She became more and more certain that people around her wanted to kill her, and she caused her mother and neighbors a good deal of grief. The family finally had her carried to a boat and taken back to the jungle hamlet where she was raised. Her mother had no faith in the city healers and wanted someone from her home to help her sick daughter. Unfortunately, the healer claimed that the woman's spirit had been captured by a witch. He was unable to help her. As I left Iquitos she remained very ill, and her baby died of pellegra.

People are quick to believe that their neighbors and relatives wish them ill, and envy them any good fortune they might have. Many different kinds of illnesses are attributed to harm (called *daño*) which is caused by another person because of motives of vengeance or envy. It is almost as if all the possible good in the world were finite and measureable. Receiving one's share in such a scheme is, in effect, cheating another of his part. One anthropologist has used the analogy of a pie in which all the good things of life are compared to a piece of pastry. As one cuts into the pie to extract a slice, it leaves just that much less for the rest of the community (see Foster, 1965). All kinds of things excite envy in Belén—a highly valued light complexion or a healthy appearance, showing that one is eating well. If a person has a loving husband or wife, if one's household is free from rancor, all kinds of malice can be provoked. A steady job netting a monthly income or being the mother of a healthy baby can cause envy in a neighbor whose husband has just lost his job or whose baby just died. In short, any kind of good luck in life can bring forth the anger of others. Getting even with a supposed wrong is also believed to be reason for harming another, especially in love matters. Many times, after a man and woman have separated and one or both have gone off to live with another person, it is thought that revenge is still desired against the former mate. Illness is then believed to follow upon the heels of such sentiment if one pays a witch. In some parts of Peru other than Iquitos, a witch may be paid to make a doll from the clothing or hair of a person who is to be the victim. This doll is then pierced with needles or cactus spines in the spot that the disease is supposed to enter. In the jungle, it is thought that *daño* is effected either through some powerful medicine which is slipped into a drink or else thrown across a doorstep late at night.

Case histories of *daño* are numerous, due to the widespread belief in the malice of people. Maria became very ill and hemorrhaged. She was told by a healer that a man she had rejected some years ago was getting his revenge. Sitting with her mother, she carefully reviewed all her past love affairs, settling upon one young man as the most probable perpetrator of her illness. Had the man lived in Belén and not back in the jungle she would never have confronted him directly with an accusation. These witchcraft activities are strong stuff indeed, and face-to-face encounters of this sort rarely take place except in the heat of anger. Maria believed her only choice was to obtain the services of another healer who could deflect the evil magic and send it back to the young man thought to be responsible for her illness.

Others like Maria fear *daño* will bring them a miserable life, prevent their spouses from being faithful, or ensure that their mate will desert the hearth.

Or else one's husband's family will hate you or you will never be able to land a spouse. Another woman claimed that her first husband's family despised her and caused her to come to harm by means of a magical potion. As she told the story, a witch had put a lump in her throat so that neither food nor water would enter her body. Fearful that she was going to die, she visited an *ayahuasquero* who was able to cure her by means of techniques of reassurance and exorcising the evil which she believed had entered her body.

Tumors, too, are often attributed to witchcraft. Don Pablo was a medical technician who made his living in Belén by giving injections and prescribing medicine. He was sure that a tumor from which he suffered was caused by his ex-wife, whom he had abandoned several years ago because, as he said, "we had a bad life together." Even though she now lived with another man, he was sure she wanted revenge and had paid a witch to make him sick. He visited several healers and finally found one he believed able to cure him. Despite the fact that he was literate, had a medical certificate from the army where he learned his trade and knowledge of modern therapeutic techniques, Pablo was as much entrenched in such magical beliefs as any of his Belén neighbors.

Consistent bad luck dogs the footsteps of many in this community. People believe that this type of bad luck doesn't happen merely by chance. Rather, the envy of people is responsible. Illness, constant aggravation, persisting difficulties, the inability to find a job—these are never attributed to individual responsibility or even abstracted to economic causes, but always to the evil willing of others. For the most part, neighbors or relatives are believed to be the guilty ones. Vultures' feces mixed with water and dropped at one's doorstep are believed able to bring about these misfortunes. Salt, too, when thrown across a middle-class neighbor's threshold or placed on the window sill is enough provocation for that person to move. Of course, if salt is placed on living plants, it can destroy whatever it touches. This contrasts to the vital role that such a substance has in maintaining life, especially in tropical climates. Yet salt is both vital and feared—it can make life possible, yet at the same time has a destructive force.

Some people believe that dead bodies are dug up so that the bones can be burned and mixed with the offal of water snakes to make a powerful, damaging charm. An illness called *saladera,* or consistent bad luck, may be caused in this manner. This syndrome is often the reason that people use ayahuasca, to find out who it is that has bewitched them, now that their life has become such a sorry affair. While under the effects of ayahuasca, a man or woman will often see a person they believe responsible for their lack of good fortune. A drama may enfold before their eyes, as a neighbor or relative appears and prepares some nasty concoction to throw before their door. It is widely believed that only a healer can deflect this evil and return it to its sender, thus removing the curse from one's person or household.

Another illness called *pulsario* is recognized by symptoms of restlessness, hyperactivity, and free-floating anxiety. Women are generally the ones who suffer this illness and cannot pay attention to one thing for any length of time, becoming irritable and feeling generally unhappy. Sometimes this malaise is described as a ball located at the mouth of their stomach, a hard lump which may be repressed pain, sorrow, or anger that cannot be expressed. One unhappily married woman, whose husband beat her and whose family lived far away, spoke of her constant anxiety and her inability to express it in any way.

Alcoholism is by no means unknown in the jungle. On a weekend day or night or holiday occasion it is not at all unusual to see men and women passed out or loud and bothersome as they drink inexpensive aguardiente in groups of noisy celebrants. However, the man or woman who consistently drinks alone, neglecting all family obligations and responsibilities, is not viewed very kindly. Family or neighborhood pressure will often motivate a suffering wife or relative to bring that person to an *ayahuasquero* to be healed. Evil sent by some vengeful or envious person who wants to cause the "alcoholic" harm rather than personal responsibility is seen as the reason for such aberrant behavior. The drug healer's role, once again, is to nullify the damage and cleanse the patient's body of all the evil bewitchment which impells him to drink.

Another illness found throughout all of Peru is called *mal de ojo,* and is similar to the evil eye of European and Middle Eastern folklore.[4] Symptoms such as nausea, vomiting, fever, loss of weight, insomnia, and sadness come about from the effects of a person's glance upon the beauty of another. Although one Peruvian medical historian, Valdivia (1964: 85), dismisses this infirmity in terms of mass paranoia, its widespread occurrence does give us some insight into levels of anxiety tied in with high mortality rates of young children, for instance, in Belén. Mothers often place amulets or charms on the wrist or neck of their babies to ward off *mal de ojo.*

The last syndrome to be described is called *despecho*—the spite or grudge held by one person against another. Here the play of human passion and disgust comes into focus, as the behavior of others is seen to be directed personally against oneself, often in the form of some kind of illness. Thus, motivation sparked by such scorn, envy, or the desire for revenge becomes responsible for magical illness. Sometimes, *despecho* may be generated for what people view as childish or immature motives. For example, a man may be held in *despecho* because he was able to gain title to a piece of land that his neighbor was hoping to obtain for himself. If the neighbor really feels strongly about the matter, he may seek out the help of a *brujo* (witch) for

---

[4]Without doubt, Spanish influence can be cited for this belief in the rain forest.

revenge. At times, all kinds of simple transactions may be seen in terms of a personal spite.

## Ayahuasca Healing and Psychosomatic Illness

*Ayahuasqueros,* like other folk healers, spend a good portion of their time using the techniques mentioned earlier in afternoon consultations, as well as visiting homes of patients to advise, counsel, and reassure. Many patients who take ayahuasca seem to be suffering from sickness that could be classified as psychosomatic. These diseases are organic malfunction of psychogenic origin, which most often results from emotional and socially precipitated stress and conflict. In many ways, psychosomatic medicine is a reaffirmation of the ancient principle that the mind and body cannot be separated and that their functions are as interactive and interdependent organs. Psychosomatic illness generally begins at a time of crisis in a patient's life. Such illness tends to disappear when situations change for the better or when the patient can learn to adapt to it without undue tension. As Hambling points out (1965: 237), psychosomatic disorders are essentially diseases of personal relationships, a fact which seems quite clear when we look at the range of culturally determined syndromes such as *susto, daño,* and *mal de ojo.* These syndromes of illness, as described to me by patients and healers in Iquitos are quite different from the taxonomy of disorders which are part of modern psychiatric analysis. As Sequin (1970: 169 ff) points out, there have been many attempts to force native-defined illnesses into different schemes closely related to Western diagnostic categories, although he believes that these attempts are unsound. Such clinical pictures cannot be treated as isolated diseases or even conceptualized apart from their own cultural background.

To the *ayahuasquero* in fact, his patient is not merely a "bearer of organs" in Franz Alexander's term (1950: 17), but an indivisible whole. Peruvian folk healers recognize the important role of emotional factors in disease, and in fact, give this great prominence in their diagnoses. One such curer and his wife laughed hard at a tale we told of a patient who suffered from love problems which medical doctors in Lima were unable to cure by prescribing medicines. To this healer, unrequited love, guilt, and similar emotional states were absolutely at the heart of a diagnosis.

## Fortunetelling Cards Used to Diagnose Illness

Luck is believed to play a very important part in peoples' lives and card-reading fortunetellers located throughout Iquitos are often visited before an important decision is made, a voyage undertaken, or a robber accused. In one of the surveys done in Iquitos, people were asked about their beliefs concerning how a person could get ahead and obtain a good job. Of the three major social segments in Iquitos, approximately 30% among the urban poor listed luck as a major factor (Wils, 1968: IV. 52). The fortunetelling cards, locally referred to as *naipes,* are not only used to predict the future, but are employed by healers as psychological aids to their therapy. Cards such as these not only attempt to determine the causality of illness, but help in elaborating the myth of the healer's omnipotence, which enables him to dispel the fears and anxieties of his patients.

In 1967, while working in the Peruvian coastal community of Valleseco, I found that both rural and urban healers used *naipes* in consultation with patients in initial phases of hallucinogenic healing. In marketplaces on the coast, and particularly in cities such as Lima and Chiclayo in the North, peddlers sold decks of cards, while badly printed booklets published in Peru and abroad were full of pictures that offered the reader the ability to predict the future.[5] Systems of card readings presented in one book were repeated verbatim in others, while completely distinctive systems appeared elsewhere claiming to be the system of a famous Italian or Spanish seer of renown. Most of the booklets agreed on basic principles. Certain days of the week are most propitious for a reading—Friday, Saturday, Tuesday, or Wednesday, for example. The client must cut the cards only with the left hand, because it is nearest to the heart, or the fortune obtained will not be accurate. The person who takes it upon himself to read the cards must not be frivolous, but sincere and strong. He also must be an observant person who washes his hands and face before using the cards. Various auguries are associated with good or bad fortune. Dropping a card while doing a reading, for example, brings bad luck.

### Historical Data on the Naipes

Printed playing cards have been traced by Kroeber to tenth century China. They appeared four centuries later, almost simultaneously, in several European countries such as Italy, Germany, and Spain. Either the Mongols or the Moslems may have transmitted such cards from China to Christian nations, despite the fact that Islam forbids all gambling.[6] Writers such as Gebelin, Singer, and Boiteau d'Ambly also cite a Chinese origin, whereas Gypsies speaking Hindustani are credited by Papus and Levi with bringing the cards from India to Europe.[7] A game of French playing cards called Tarot, used in

---

[5]See in particular LeNormand (n.d.); Anon. (n.d.); Anon. (1957); Segura and Sanjaman (1956); Silva et al. (1965).
[6]Kroeber (1948: 495).
[7]Gebelin (1781); Singer (1816); Boiteau d'Ambly (1954); Papus (1891); Levi (1920).

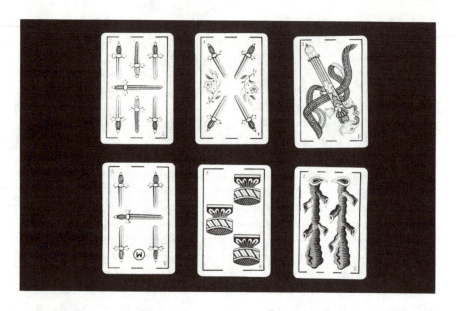

Fortunetelling cards, locally called **naipes,** are used not only to predict the future but are employed by healers as psychological aids in their therapy.

divination and popular during the Middle Ages, was believed to have resulted from an adaptation of a card game called *Naibi* to which was added a series of point cards.[8] The original Tarot cards have been linked to the esoteric Jewish Kabbalah tradition, with the twenty-two major Tarot cards said to be related to the letters of the Hebrew alphabet. The game *Naibi* (also referred to as *Nayb*)[9] was known in Italy during the fourteenth century.

In the Dictionary of the Royal Spanish Academy, the term *naipes* is etymologically derived from the Arab *naib,* he who represents, or *laib,* he who plays.[10] If playing cards used in divination were known in fourteenth century Spain, it would not be at all difficult to trace the movement of such divinatory aids to the New World, despite the lack of historical documentation. Certainly, the period of the Conquest was one in which men seeking adventure and wealth in unknown lands might be expected to take gaming cards along with them. A deck of forty-eight cards, small and easily portable, no doubt found its way into the Hispanic world at the time of the sixteenth century conquest. Indeed, Garcilaso de la Vega's book, published in the mid seventeenth century, has a drawing showing abuses practiced by members of the clergy who gamed at cards.[11] In a way that at best can remain a matter of speculation only, these cards became syncretized into Peruvian folk healing and hallucinogenic healing. Today, the cards are used throughout Latin America, not only for fortunetelling but for entertainment and gambling as well.

## Some Comments on Folk Medicine

As we have seen in this chapter, in Peru, as in many other areas of the world undergoing rapid cultural change, there are folk healers who treat a large number of psychosomatic disorders. Dr. Oscar Rios, a Peruvian psychiatrist who observed a folk-healing session in northeastern Peru prior to 1967, made a presumptive diagnosis in which some 85% of the patients in attendance suffered from psychiatric or psychosomatic illness. Many of the studies on traditional psychiatry today (see Kiev, 1968; Plog, 1969) show quite clearly that native healers are most effective when there are psychosomatic and other psychological disturbances precipitated by some social complication. While Western-trained medical personnel tend to anticipate a physical cause for most ailments, native folk healers, as in Peru, may very well be in a position to be more effective if their training and judgment from past experience predispose

---

[8]Spence (1920).
[9]Van Rijnberg (1947).
[10]Diccionario de la Lengua Española (1956).
[11](1961: 351).

them toward a higher expectation of emotionally and culturally precipitated illness.

Treatment by folk healers throughout the world is based on the prestige, reassurance, and suggestion that the healer can offer his patients. The use of a divinatory technique such as that of the *naipes* can tap the culturally-induced stresses that are contributory to illness in many cases. A healer utilizing such a technique can "remove the agency and responsibility for a decision from the sick person and cast it upon the heavens ... When this procedure is combined with ritual, attitudes toward the diviner and his paraphernalia are reaffirmed" (Park, 1967: 236). A divination technique, if cleverly manipulated by a healer, can permit an understanding of the source of disorder, which may be seen by the healer to be part of conflict-filled and anxiety-laden social relationships.

Throughout the following analysis of the *naipes,* I will try to point up the way that interpersonal tensions, anxieties, and conflicts—all important etiological components of illness—can be ferreted out by the divining healer in his diagnostic techniques. By manipulation of a category present in the *naipes* that I have elsewhere labeled misfortune cards[12], the healer can plumb the depths of interpersonal conflicts, material loss, sickness or death of a loved one to make his diagnosis.

### Fortune's Malice in the Peruvian Rain Forest

In Belén, many men and women consult folk healers, known as *curiosos,* who read the *naipes.* Given the importance of *daño* as a major etiological category considered responsible for different illnesses ranging in effect from muscular ache to loss of consciousness and madness, the cards are very informative to a sick person. There are, for example, twelve cards that represent individuals of a particular physical appearance, which can be used to identify a man or woman believed responsible for misfortune or bewitchment. Thus, a card such as the ace of spades or the four of spades (in one reading system believed to signify envy, jealousy, or bad intentions) followed by a man or woman can be construed by the reader to touch upon a sensitive area of disease causality. A sick woman suffering from startle fright *(susto)* after her husband abandoned her, may consult a healer to ask if her husband will return. Frightened of the magical damage that her common-law spouse's former wife can cause her, a woman may turn to the cards for reassurance, perhaps even for help in deciding whether to leave her spouse. Marriage counseling and insight into the cause of physical and emotional illness set within a magical framework are readily amenable to the divining cards.

My own use of the *naipes* as a general ethnographic aid not only helped

---

[12]See Dobkin de Rios (1969c).

establish rapport with members of the community but reaffirmed many of my own impressions about the stresses and strains that emerged from my day-to-day experiences. Many of the questions which clients could ask after a particular reading brought up tabooed topics difficult to discuss beforehand. Figure cards representing men and women of distinctive physical appearance were interpreted by my clients to be particular members of their family or friends whom they believed intervened and contributed to their luck. Many women expressed great fear of being abandoned by their spouses or of being left alone to rear their children without their husband's economic support. Relationships between men and women appeared to be full of distrust. Others confided their desire to travel to distant areas in search of work or job security. Areas of concern such as economic security or desire for wealth appeared in conversations about the readings. Throughout all the readings, remarks focusing upon distrust of neighbors and relatives, lack of self confidence, adulterous temptations and activities, and intimate values in love and courtship appeared, while interpersonal strife and conflict, desire for children, and fear of illness were recurrent themes. When, in accordance with books of instruction, I would weave general category cards such as money, fate, happiness, bad treatment, debts, suffering, etc. into general stories whose purpose and details were left vague, this would serve to stimulate and trigger confidences that many prior months of fieldwork had not managed to tap (see Dobkin de Rios, 1971).

Perhaps the major benefit of my somewhat unconventional role was eliciting the prominant focus that ayahuasca had in evil activities by witches. Many people discussed with me the details of their past or present illnesses, which they were certain had been precipitated by evildoers who received money for their services.

## Witches Who Use Ayahuasca for Evil

Although I have so far discussed the use of ayahuasca in healing activities, not all people who use the vine do so merely to benefit others. Many, in fact, known as *brujos,* or witches, attempt to use the purge in order to harm. Sought out by men and women motivated by envy, desire for vengeance, or hatred of others, they are asked to damage, obtain revenge, or to bring illness and bad fortune to despised individuals. During the year I spent in Belén, I met and talked to a few witches who were pointed out to me by people in the community. In some ways, their activities coincided with other healers I knew and interviewed. People with love problems came to them for *pusangas* or other charms to bewitch a man they loved or perhaps make an errant husband or wife return. Clients who thought they had been bewitched visited these men just as they might any other *ayahuasquero.* Using techniques such as sucking, singing, whistling, and blowing tobacco smoke over the sick person, these *brujos* effected some cures. Evil-doing, however, was their speciality. One man, originally from Brazil, had a terrible reputation. It was rumored that he had learned occult arts in Manaus. A very suspicious person and uneasy among people whom he felt lacked confidence in him, he was feared for his great powers and was quick to suspect that people were trying to "get something on him" in order to bring charges before the police.

Although many ayahuasca healers protest that they are not themselves witches, they often will tell of people who seek their services in order to cause magical harm to others. Many refuse, and the patients who solicited them merely keep on looking for someone who has a reputation for evil doing. Jungle folklore is full of accounts of witches' behavior. One Amazonian novelist, Arturo Hernandez, has written about a jungle farmer who learned to use ayahuasca for evil purposes.

In the full moon, Alfonso began to take his potion, singing the forbidden *Bubinzana* song (of bewitchment) with mystical dedication, invoking powers whose existence he vaguely felt. One night he believed he saw something descend from the atmosphere upon him. Another evening he took his drink under the impression that something extraordinary was going to happen. A little afterwards, he felt he was leaving his earthly shell and saw himself floating in space close to light, ethereal transparent forms, which possessed a great mobility. He noted with surprise that he, himself, was one of these forms, but unlike the rest, he remained immobile. He didn't take long to realize that he had penetrated a world as infinite as the cosmos, the world of the spirits, negated by sceptics in spite of their multiple manifestations, but admitted by the primitive men who intuitively felt that which they encountered outside of their sense and negating reason (1960: 27).

After a solitary life in which Alfonso mourns the death of his beloved who was carried off to the land below the water, this lonely man repeatedly took ayahuasca in an attempt to communicate with his lost Clothilde. During the course of several full moons, the man came to recognize the guardian spirits of flowers and fruits whom he encountered while under the effects of the purge. But he still felt a desire for revenge against the father of Clothilde, who tried to make his daughter marry someone else against her will, forcing the lovers to run away through dense forest in a journey that nearly killed both of them. Alfonso began to plan his revenge. One night while under the effects of ayahuasca, he had the experience of leaving his body to take his revenge: "He found the father of Clothilde in a deep sleep, sweating with his belly uncovered . . . And Alfonso penetrated him very deeply in this palpitating belly as wild beasts grabbed their victims with poisonous claws. But it was not poison that Alfonso left in him, but much worse—it was an evil the witch controlled, which produced unknown and incurable illness (*Ibid.:* 124)." Alfonso then visited the home of the man who was to marry Clothilde. He entered his genitalia, causing them to swell to fearsome proportions. Both the father and betrothed of the girl called in all the village healers but could not be cured by any treatment.

It is perhaps unfortunate that one must look to literature to describe the nature of evil as it is elaborated in rain forest witchcraft, since this aspect of data gathering is difficult to verify on an empirical basis. Few if any *ayahuasqueros* will admit to being witches (see Dobkin de Rios, 1970). While drinking with friends in confidence, some may reluctantly tell of their apprenticeship to a healer, and their fright and dismay when they were told that to become a powerful curer they would have to kill as well as heal. For example, a violinist in Belén who played at birthday parties and funerals wanted to be an *ayahuasquero* in his youth. But a time came when his teacher insisted that he would have to perform evil magic to complete his training. Jorge gave up in dismay at the thought of poisoning someone or trying to cause a death by casting a spell. Despite the compunctions of a few, jungle communities are full of tales of people who somehow offended a man or woman believed to be knowledgeable in these areas. As the tales generally go, the offending person suddenly died within a few days.

Two different kinds of mechanisms seem to account for this type of rapid death. Without doubt, when a person believes that he has been bewitched, he may go into a state of shock and die, as Cannon has reported for Voodoo death (1942: 168–169). That author, for example, has described in physiological terms how fear by itself may be responsible for illness and even death, since both fear and rage have similar effects on the human organism and can bring the sympathetic nervous system into special action. To be more specific, when the body is stimulated by great fear, the action of the heart and other organs under the control of the sympathetic nervous system are greatly accelerated. Blood vessels contract, the liver releases great quantities of blood sugar, and the adrenal glands send large amounts of adrenaline into the system. Should such a condition prevail over a long period of time, blood pressure lowers and the patient dies. A person in the rain forest who fears he has been bewitched may frantically approach a healer whom he believes possesses counter magic powerful enough to deflect the evil in an effort to relieve the constant anxiety which torments him.

Another possibility accounting for magical death may be that of hardcore poisoning. Scores of jungle plants exist which when carefully prepared and introduced into a drink or food, or placed on a person's body, can kill quickly and quietly. If a witch were disposed to discuss his techniques, it would no doubt include either suggestive phenomena or the use of killer plants. However, from the point of view of the fearful victim or his family, these techniques are intricately linked under the notion of "the witch's power." The rain forest is an area of the world possessing an immense number of plant poisons. One anthropologist writing of a primitive horticultural group who utilizes ayahuasca, mentions some thirty-six poisonous plants that his group knew and probably used. Some of these kill quickly while others when dried produce diarrhea, blood excretion, and a slow wasting away. Another plant poison swells the abdomen until it bursts while still another plant is too poisonous even to be touched. This group, the Cubeo, make an infusion of the plant which can cause a person who touches it to die. In fact, a series of illnesses from poisons leading to death is common knowledge among them.[13] It is not difficult to imagine that much knowledge concerning destructive botanical materials have survived among Mestizo and *Cholo* populations whose mode of exploiting the rain forest environment is not far removed from primitive horticultural groups like the Cubeo.

### Witchcraft: Functional or Dysfunctional?

We have looked at some of the evidence for witchcraft beliefs, as well as examined different kinds of illness and motivation for harming others, and we really should stop for a moment and ask some basic questions about the functional or dysfunctional effects of such behavior. For many years, anthropologists studying societies where complicated beliefs in witchcraft existed have tried to explain away and justify such seemingly irrational and unproductive behavior by looking for some positive benefit accruing to the members of the social group.[14] For example, one reads that witchcraft beliefs offered primitive society explanations for the unknown, for the ubiquitous threat of illness, or else asked different kinds of questions for which modern science might have no rationale, especially when conflict with others was a commonplace occurrence. Explanations for misfortune attributed to witchcraft beliefs have been viewed as concrete personifications of causality, which permit reduction of anxiety and the resumption of normal social life. One writer, Evans-Pritchard (1937), has been quick to point out that once the basic premises of such beliefs are accepted, witchcraft systems have an inherent logic of their own and often contain logically intricate systems of thought. Some writers believe that societies with witchcraft beliefs are able to translate the diffused and paralyzing effect of anxiety into fear, which can then be dealt with somewhat more rationally. Witchcraft beliefs are thus seen to be either adaptive or adjustive, the latter occurring especially when beliefs in witches may cause a group of people to unite in order to destroy the evil-doers in their midst (see Kluckhohn, 1944: 85 ff). Among the urban poor in Belén, this has never been reported. Perhaps the best that can be said for witchcraft beliefs in Belén is that pent-up emotions become dissolved in a socially harmless way.

---

[13]See Goldman (1963: 268).
[14]See Kluckhohn (1944).

Yet despite these varied attempts to find some positive function in systems of belief with an acceptance of personal malice in different primitive and peasant societies around the world, there are in fact many dysfunctional aspects of such beliefs that must be considered. One writer, John G. Kennedy (1970), has pointed out how witchcraft systems seem closely similar to paranoid delusions, as they provide a paranoid view of the world. Such a world view has people projecting their innermost feelings and seeing others as basically evil persons who wish to do them harm. Motives such as jealousy, envy, desire for vengeance, scorn, spite and the like surround the individual as he goes about his daily routine. Certainly in the realm of illness, somatic ailments may come about from this persistent psychic stress. As Kennedy states, "knowing that someone wants to kill you and seems to be having apparent success in conjunction with a given organic pain, does not help very much in healing" (*Ibid.*: 14). Stress built into a given community's social system must be viewed as it impinges upon and impairs functioning by members of that community.

The example of Belén stands out here. Belén is a community torn with strife and envy, despair, hopelessness, and aggression, as the many fist fights and hair-pulling spectacles which bring neighbors running to the street can attest. Ayahuasca enters the picture as one way in which healers can ameliorate and relieve some of these daily pressures which, of course, effect particular people differently. The threshold of endurance certainly varies from person to person and factors such as life circumstances and the kinds of daily stresses to which a person is subject and with which he must learn to cope become very important to keep in mind. Organic pain, impaired body functioning, free-floating anxiety, all cathect and become identified as someone else's evil wishing. Simple cures may be sought, e.g., having smoke blown over one's body or listening to special orations and songs to deflect the evil magic, but if all this fails, recourse to the powerful purge—ayahuasca—will enable one to see exactly who it is who is responsible for one's bewitchment. A wise healer who can deflect evil magic under such circumstances becomes a necessity. Perhaps the way in which this jungle community deals with problems of magical beliefs by using ayahuasca sets it apart from the dozens of other areas around the world where healers find other ways to work their counter-magic to protect sick patients from the malice of others.

# Ayahuasca Healers and Patients: Biographies

# 7

In the following pages, we will look at the background of several *ayahuasqueros* and their patients in some detail. In presenting these biographies, I have tried to convey a picture of healers and clients who are numbered both from among the poorest, most illiterate members of the community to men and women of better education and more secure economic status.

## Four Healers

Don Antonio: This healer, a man in his early forties, lived in a two room balsa house with his wife and four children. He was about 5 feet 2 inches tall and could fade easily into a crowd, as he was undistinguished in appearance. He was always dressed in patched shirts and baggy trousers, since outward signs of success were not important to him. Although he did not appear to be particularly well-off financially (see photograph), he had a jungle farm some four days journey away. His house contained only a tiny back room and an open porch. In the patio area, a woolen blanket was hung across a slung wire to provide a consultation area and to give him some privacy where he would sit perhaps with a mother and her sick baby, a parent and her adolescent daughter, or a man and his wife suffering from some love problem. Healing in the late afternoon without drugs, he would blow *mapacho* smoke over the sick, as he whistled special incantations in accordance with the type of illness. Visiting some of his more incapacitated patients in the mornings, Antonio would spend a good deal of time away from home as he made his daily rounds. Like other healers, Antonio generally received his fee after he affected a cure. Often he would see little money from the destitute poor that he treated. Herbs, plants and medicines were his speciality, and he would prepare particular potions for different patients. The ayahuasca he used was brought to him for cash by some men he knew in Belén. He also used a leaf called *Chacruna* (most probably containing N-N-Dimethyltryptamine; see der Marderosian, 1968) which was another powerful hallucinogen that he added to his healing drink at the boiling stage. Tuesday, Thursday, and Saturday nights were set aside by him for healing, although rain often would cause postponement to another evening. On occasion, he might hold the healing session in the balsa hut of a fisherman friend, especially if it were too late to go to one of the several jungle clearings that he preferred, about an hour and a half's distance from his home. Most of his clients were recommended to him by friends or relatives of people he had cured. Like most other healers, he carefully selected the patients he agreed to cure with ayahuasca, only one of the healing techniques he used. Many of his clients came to him with simple aches, pains, fevers, upset stomachs, parasitical complaints, and the like. A quiet man, not much given to boasting, Antonio would occasionally speak of those he had cured, their problems, symptoms, pains, who had bewitched them and caused them harm. He married at thirty (rather late in life for this region) after spending two years as an apprentice to a famous jungle healer. Living in the *monte,* or uninhabited rain forest and subsisting on mouthfuls of food, he learned to take ayahuasca regularly and control its effects upon his body. He became familiar with the various medicinal herbs which grew in the rain forest as he prepared remedies and salves for different ailments. Today, on holiday occasions such as Christmas, when he returns to his jungle hamlet, his neighbors hail him as a local dignitary. Once functioning as the administrative head of the hamlet, he is *compadre* to most of the men of the village after taking on the obligation of godfather to their children at birth or first communion. A religious bond of kinship is created on such occasions between the godfather and parents of the child involved. As godfather to most of the youngsters in this community, he is called upon to heal his godchildren without charge, although in return he receives gifts of food.

His eldest daughter is in high school, which is no mean accomplishment for most families in Belén. Uniforms and books are costly, especially when youngsters' earnings are unavailable to the family income. Elvira hopes to become a schoolteacher some day. Her parents, however, are anxious to see her marry a young man from back home who has been courting her. Resentful and unwilling to marry him because he is a *Cholo,* she thinks, she despises his dark skin and lack of smooth city ways. Her mother is concerned by her daughter's

An **Ayahuascero's** house in Belén, where
he receives his clients.

stubbornness, since apparently the young man has been generous and helpful
to the family. Neither Antonio nor his wife, however, will force their child to
marry, preferring instead to use gentle persuasion.

In making any kind of judgment about Antonio's abilities, one must ac-
knowledge that he is in some respects inept when compared with other healers.
His songs and whistling incantations are rather mediocre. At times, he seemed
quite ineffective in his sessions. Once, when I was present, he neglected to
prepare enough ayahuasca for the number of people who came to the session.
A couple who came to him for marital counseling because of the husband's
irrational jealousy paid little attention to Antonio that evening. This session,
unlike others, ended at about 11 P.M., since no one seemed to be feeling the
effects of the poorly prepared drink. In addition, Antonio's sloppy, tattered
clothes and flimsy balsa house would appear to place him among the poorest
in the community, although some subtleties show his certain success. For
example, his wife has a well-oiled sewing machine, paid for on credit, which
is put to constant use for her family's clothing. All of Antonio's children attend
school and he owns a fair-sized parcel of land back in the jungle. Occasional
chickens adorn his table and his daughter doesn't have to work to help support
the family. Like many in Belén, Antonio and his wife realize that once their

daughter were to leave home to work as a shopgirl in the city, she would suffer from discrimination in subtle ways, or else be exploited sexually by a supervisor or boss. Needless to say, her parents do not find this pleasant to consider. It may very well be that in some dark corner of his house Antonio has hidden money away for a rainy day. Although it appears that he lives a hand-to-mouth existence, he does in fact seem to be much better off than many of his neighbors, who when dawn comes often do not know where their next meal will come from. Certainly, Antonio does not have to work at a hundred and one different odd jobs in the hopes of staying alive as do many of his neighbors. Clients seek him out and he can count on a fair, although unpredictable income. Most of his clients seem to come from other poverty-striken communities in Iquitos.

Don Carlos: This healer, too, is not a native of Belén, but originally from a jungle hamlet called Tamishiyacu some six hours away. His house in Belén is poorly built, but Carlos is boastful of the house he had planned to build before the famous fire of 1965 destroyed his *choza* (hut) and a trunk where he had saved over $700 in small bills. Don Carlos has little faith in city ways, such as the cooperative loan society at the edge of the city, which builds up capital from the pittance of poor people, while lending to wealthy merchants at low interest rates for purposes of business expansion.

Fear of the police haunts Carlos' thoughts, and although he doesn't admit to it, he must have had some problems in his youth. At the age of sixty-five, he has managed to give his three sons a secondary education. They now have their own farms and provide him with a daily pension. Like other healers, he is proud of the time he was apprenticed to an *ayahuasquero* and spent a few years in the *monte*, learning about different hallucinogenic plants with the help of his teacher. During this period, he ate very little and went without salt. Needless to say, in a tropical area, salt pays a very essential part in body metabolism. Limiting salt intake is commonly practiced by ayahuasca apprentices.

Carlos, like most *ayahuasqueros*, does not accept all those patients who seek him out, but is careful in his selection. He prefers to work with small groups since the atmosphere created tends to be a better one that way than it is among a group of twenty to thirty people (which he says money-hungry healers prefer). During his years of military service, Carlos treated many soldiers who believed they suffered from *daño*, especially after military doctors were unable to do anything for them. His superior officers knew of his activities, but made no attempt to stop him, rather relieved, it appeared in the telling, that someone had success with soldiers stationed in the rain forest, who suffered from afflictions that modern medicine could not cure.

Don Carlos can be characterized as a die-hard conservative who frequently harkens back to the good old days when life was more predictable and men and women behaved differently. In fact, many folk healers could hardly be classified as progressively oriented members of their community. Their charter to cure stems from long established traditions. Such healers often see both changing times and medical personnel as a threat, although they may be quick to incorporate into their curing kit the benefits of penicillin, antibiotics, or other pharmaceutical medicines.

Like Antonio, Carlos collects a fee from his patients only after he has been successful. No initial payments are demanded by him. This compares drastically to the behavior of witches, who are notorious in seeking a large downpayment before they begin their work. Many healers like Carlos are extremely effective in commercially-minded communities like Belén, where everything has economic referents. By not demanding payment until some progress has been made and a patient is better able to work again to pay his debts, the healer is quite apt to establish easily a relationship of trust. Generally the gratitude a patient feels at being cured makes him a relatively good "credit risk," although many do in fact default. Healers are often left with bitter memories of patients whom they cured who did not pay their bills.

An excellent judge of people and very much aware of the high levels of anxiety and stress which mark the day-to-day existence of people in this jungle community, Carlos spoke at length of the daily desires of his clients to get even with someone or to take revenge on a neighbor or relative whom they believe harmed them. He talked about the fear of magical bewitchment which springs to a person's mind the moment he feels ill. Many kinds of evil medicines are used against his patients, he claimed, to cause the sickness or bad luck that he is called upon to remedy. Unlike Antonio, don Carlos claimed to be a devout Catholic. At one session that Antonio conducted, a woman shouted, "Oh God, help me," as her visions filled with frightening creatures. Antonio told her that the name of Jesus Christ had no place in the magical circle we had formed and cautioned her not to repeat that phrase again. Carlos, on the other hand, considers his gift of healing directly due to God's grace. Speaking almost in terms of a bargain that he made with God, Carlos stressed that beginning at 6 A.M. on Sunday, he does not work, so as to observe the sabbath; nor will he permit sick patients to visit him on this day. During the time I knew him, he was treating two members of a family with whom I was quite friendly. Phenomenal success marked his dealings with the mother, doña Teresa, whose case I will talk about shortly. Carlos was unable to be of any help, however, to her daughter Norma, a girl of eighteen, who suffered from epilepsy (called *mal de gota*). After she had unsuccessfully taken ayahuasca twice, Norma had to travel with her mother to Brazil to see about some family property. During a convulsion, the young woman fell into the river and drowned.

Don José: Living in a small suburb of Iquitos near a military post, this healer has a home which was much more substantial than that of his other two colleagues. In contrast to the flimsy woven bark walls or balsa raft flooring and mud-baked walls so common in Belén, don José's residence was constructed of wooden plank board and had a cemented floor. Instead of a thatched roof (which is a fire hazard and has to be replaced every few years), his was of calamine, a durable zinc-like material which lasts a lifetime. Adjacent to the house, which was on the Itaya River (a small inlet feeding into the Amazon), he docked his own boat, although he stored his American motor inside his house for safety's sake. Having a boat enabled him to make frequent trips to a little farm he owned about an hour's journey up river, where he grew his own psychedelic plants that he used in curing, including a tree called *toé (Datura suavoleons)*. He was very knowledgeable about many different hallucinogenic plants, including *ayahuaman* (unidentified) and a trance-inducing tobacco *(nicotiana tabacum?)*, all of which he used in healing. Doctors from the Institute of Social Psychiatry in Lima had made contact with him some months prior to my stay, and requested preparations which I helped ship from Iquitos to be used in animal experiments.

The interior of José's house, too, was much more substantial than those of other Belén healers' houses, as he was a fairly successful curer. His specialty was afternoon sessions in which abandoned wives would come to him for help. He took ayahuasca in order to "capture" the soul of the man who had left, and he boasted he would be able to bring him back to his wife within a month's time. Patients also visited him during late afternoons, at which time, like others in his profession, he would blow cigarette smoke over their bodies and pre-scribe herbs and pharmaceutical medicines for them to use. It wasn't necessary for his wife to work at a market stall as did many of her neighbors, since don José had few problems about ready cash. Ayahuasca healing kept him busy two or three nights a week, depending upon the number of patients who came to him, and his ritual songs and whistling were a treat to hear. Tall and lean, about fifty-five years old, he would boastfully discuss his patients and the many successes for which he was famous. When asked about retiring to the *monte* during the month of August as do many healers in order to renew their strength and seek protection against the evil magic of others who envy them their successes, don José was quick to point out that although many of his patients believed in *daño,* or magical harm, he did not. As a result, he was sure that jealous healers could cause him no danger. People believe that good healers die young because they are killed by deceitful, envious witches. When asked how he diagnosed and cured illness, José stressed the fact that he had knowledge from a particular kind of science, all of which came from a book reputed to have been written by St. Ciprian, the patron saint of Peruvian folk healers. As the legend goes, before Ciprian was converted to Christianity, in the first century A.D., he was one of the best known magicians in the Roman world. He had absolute dominion over evil spirits, who would obey his every command. When he was asked to effect love magic on a young Christian woman by a man who was in love with her, Ciprian was unable to succeed since the girl placed herself under the protection of the Virgin Mary. She managed to resist Ciprian's evil by protecting herself with the cross of St. Bartholomy and the grace of Jesus. Ciprian was infuriated by his inability to work his spell on the woman and conjured up Lucifer, who told him that the god of the Christians was the God of all created. Ciprian converted to Christianity, was martyred, and became a saint. He is much admired throughout Peru, and coastal healers who use mescaline in their healing arts often maintain chapels in his name.

José said that he depended a good deal on this Saint, particularly for his orations and preparations of curative herbs. Yet José knew very little of the actual biography of Ciprian, which was printed in several inexpensive paperback folios for sale in marketplaces. Although some of José's comments appeared to me to be those of a charlatan, I suppose his sincerity should be viewed in terms of his effectiveness in healing. Certainly, influences from medical science stemming from radio and newspapers which were available to him found their way into his conversation, which was interspersed with scientific terminology.

Don Federico: This last healer to be discussed seemed to me to be the wealthiest and perhaps the best known of the *ayahuasqueros* I met. A man of about sixty, he lived about five miles from the center of town in a recently built-up working class neighborhood. A city housing project faced his well-built, wooden slate-board and calamine-roofed house. His immense front room was of ballroom proportions compared to the many dingy houses of wooden construction found in Belén and the other areas of the city. Federico's wife, Yolanda, was a charming, well-informed ayahuasca healer in her own right, working hand-in-hand with her husband in taking the purge, and adding her voice to the incantations sung for sick people. She was a little older than the wives of the other healers I had met, and was outspoken and boastful of the many patients her husband had cured. In the past, don Federico had gathered his patients together to hold their healing sessions in the jungle clearings, but now with the recent construction of his fine house he set up shop in his spacious backyard. This faced a wooded area and was fairly quiet. The new housing development had not as yet opened, and the streets were quiet, protecting the session from unwelcomed noises of barking dogs, yelling children, or gossiping neighbors.

Federico's sessions were much larger in scale than any of the others I attended during my stay in Iquitos. As the healer's fame had spread throughout the city, he worked not the traditional schedule of Tuesday, Thursday, and Saturday, but Mondays, Wednesdays, and Fridays. His backyard filled with an average of twenty-five patients each of these evenings. They were generally seated in a circle that extended over a rather large area so that one could not actually see all the people who were taking ayahuasca. Several hallucinogenic plants were used in preparing his drink. Depending upon the nature of the illness afflicting a particular patient, the healer would also prepare a special potion to be taken. Sessions started quite late, and were attended by poor jungle peasants, middle class housewives, rich businessmen, and occasional professional townspeople who took the drug not for any magical harm they suffered but rather for enjoyment, on a steady weekly basis. Don Federico's fame was such that he had several young college students from the local university serving him as apprentices. They visited him periodically to take the purge and learn its healing ways. Later on, some of them might become healers in their own right. As with don José, Federico, too, raised his own mind-altering plants, preferring this method instead of depending upon fishermen or travelers to bring him the needed plants. Since his sessions were so well attended, he was sure to have plenty of the purge on hand. Nonetheless, if a sick man or woman wished to find out the cause of his infirmity by taking ayahuasca, he would not merely show up at Federico's house. He would probably see the healer first in the late afternoon and make an appointment to come back. Federico might then exorcise the prospective patient during one or two preparatory sessions before he actually invited that patient to drink the potion. In these first sessions, after everyone else had taken ayahuasca, Federico would go around the circle, singing, chanting, whistling, and shaking his *schacapa* rattle over each person for at least ten to twenty minutes. Later in the evening, he would discuss problems and counsel each man and woman in turn about their medical problems. It was quite apparent that he prepared future ayahuasca drinkers for their entry into the magical realm that he guided, as he discussed *daño,* the evil of people, and how the purge worked. He talked of his successes in deflecting and returning evil magic to the responsible wrongdoer, and boasted of how he had cured such and such a person of the very same illness. Finally, when the moment of actual drug experience came for this patient at another date, it took on the quality of a *déja-vu* or expected experience for which careful groundwork had been laid.

Don Federico did not seem to be a wealthy man. Yet, he owned his land and house, had expensive, well-made wooden furniture in his parlor, a well-stocked kitchen with store-bought kerosene stoves for his wife, and a sewing machine. His son rode an expensive bicycle. Although he and his wife dressed simply, it was believed that they had accumulated savings. Since Federico's fame was widespread, his fees for healing were almost comparable to city doctors, although still somewhat cheaper. One patient who said the city hospital wanted $150 to operate on her for an ovarian cyst was told by Federico she could be cured by him for half the price. He said an operation was not necessary since her illness was caused by magical harm, which was sent to her by her ex-husband's current wife. Herbs and special preparations would be part of the treatment, and she was instructed to attend several sessions in the healer's house. In addition, she was told to bring her three children along on one visit, so that they could be protected from future harm by having *mapacho* smoke blown over them as a prevention from whatever evil the same woman might cause.

## Ayahuasca Patients

Manuela: A jungle migrant to Belén, this elderly woman believed very strongly in the power of magical beings which inhabit both forest and river. She lived with two of her daughters in a floating balsa house and had a terrible time staying alive. Whenever she had some money she would spend long hours down by the dock, waiting for boats to come in, loaded with fish, vegetables, or rice. At times, when foodstuffs were not plentiful, she would have to push and shove to get a place up front in the crowd of women vying for available produce. Fortunately, two of her unmarried children worked as shopgirls in Iquitos, and were able to help support her with some of their earnings.

When she lived back in a jungle hamlet some seven years ago she became ill one day with a hemorrhage. Certain that her illness was caused by the mother spirit of the jungle, she was convinced she had been punished for violating a taboo concerning menstruation. During her menstrual period she went into the forest one day to gather palm leaves to weave into a new roof for her hut. She was wrong, she now thought, to have entered the forest while she was menstruating. For this reason, she was punished by the forest spirit. Her family took her to a local *ayahuasquero* to be healed. He blew tobacco smoke over her and prescribed a series of herbs that she took during a two-week period. Manuela often joined in discussion about ayahuasca and the people who looked for help from the drug. Interestingly enough, in the community where she grew up, she received a religious education, as the Catholic Church had an active mission program in some of the scattered hamlets. Once, while I was discussing a particular ayahuasca session I had attended she cautioned me that healers who spent too much time with the spirits will not be able to see the face of Jesus Christ when they die. Some kind of conflict apparently existed for her in reconciling the powerful jungle guardian spirits of nature in which she believed with her religious training. Like many others women in the community, she lived in a common-law union for many years. She was quite anxious, however, to be married in the Church before she died.

As one priest put it to her all too succinctly, if jungle farmers did not marry, they were no better than the monkeys who ran loose in the forest.

Rosa: A handsome woman of thirty-eight, Rosa had four children with whom she lived. Her second husband, Julio, worked as a fisherman. When Rosa was eighteen and lived in a jungle hamlet near the Brazilian border, she suddenly became a secret alcoholic. Without telling anyone in her family, she would slyly drink about two pints of cane alcohol *(aguardiente)* a day. Although she didn't lose her virginity at that time, her drinking somehow came to the attention of her family. An anxious aunt took her to a community *ayahuasquero* for help. Under the effects of the drug, she saw a drama unfolding before her, in which a young man she knew proposed they live together as man and wife. Mirroring events which had indeed happened to her, the visions showed her refusing the boy, because as she recalled, he was irresponsible and hadn't served his two years in the army. Without doubt, she thought, he would just bring her *la mala vida* if she went to live with him now. Under the effects of ayahuasca, she saw the rejected suitor reappear before her, wanting revenge for being spurned. As her visions changed, she saw a party which she attended shortly thereafter come into focus. During the celebration, the boy secretly prepared a white powder and slipped it into her *chicha* (a fermented corn drink). This powder caused her to become an alcoholic. When she told the healer of her visual experiences, he interpreted to her the various details concerning her bewitchment. He told Rosa he would return the evil to the young man. Within a relatively short time it became known that the boy had fought with his family and was thrown out of his house, never to return again. Rosa gave up drinking and had no occasion to consult a healer for many years.

When Rosa and I talked about this experience, I asked her if the healer might have punished the young man more severely than he did, perhaps inflicting some illness upon him. Rosa replied that of course this could have been done, but she was not a really spiteful person and did not care to see him harmed. Had she been such a person, she said, she might indeed have looked for magical help to bring about the boy's death or cause him grave physical harm.

Pedro: A carpenter by trade, Pedro, at twenty-three, lived in one of the squatter settlements surrounding Iquitos. He asked for help of a healer in Belén to cure him of *saladera*. For over two years, he hadn't been able to get any steady work and had had bad luck with women. Nothing, in fact, seemed to go right for him. Suspecting that someone was bewitching him, he went to an *ayahuasquero* for help. While under the effects of the drug, he saw a former friend of his with whom he had worked building *colectivos,* those small passenger and cargo boats that ply the rivers, serving hundreds of hamlets and small farms down river. His friend, José, appeared before him, full of envy for his carpentry skills. Quickly thereafter he had another vision in which José appeared before his door, throwing an evil concoction in order to bewitch him. The healer helped Pedro interpret his visions, and said he would return the evil magic to the man who was responsible. Within a short time things had changed considerably for Pedro. He got a commission to build a large *colectivo,* and his uncle went into partnership with him and put up the capital so that he would be able to start working.

Berta: A woman of thirty-seven who had nine children, Berta spoke of a time not so long ago when she and her husband lived back in a jungle hamlet. She worked as a cook in a local market center. After being happily married for several years, with a hard-working husband who treated her and the youngsters well, Berta suddenly found herself wanting to respond to the sexual advances of an older man. He was a pensioner for whom she cooked, and he wanted her to leave her husband and run off to live with him. Berta spoke to her husband, and they both went to an *ayahuasquero.* She had to take ayahuasca seven times that evening before any visions appeared, but she finally saw this older man give her a potion which caused her to want to return his sexual advances. The vision was duly reported to the healer who interpreted Berta's sudden sexual interest in the man as pure bewitchment. When her *compadre* learned of the results of the healing session, he threw the older man out of the house and threatened him with bodily harm if he ever returned. In this case, a happy marriage was viewed as worth holding on to, and fickle sexual desire for another was seen as the obvious result of evil magic.

Gloria: A young woman who grew up in Belén, Gloria went off to live with a *rematista* at the age of fourteen. He traveled a good deal but was a fairly good husband to her. Although I used to see her frequently, as we were neighbors, she invariably mentioned that three of her four children had died in infancy. When Gloria was twenty-one, her husband became bored with her and set up another household in a different part of Belén with a much younger girl. As her mother tells the story, Gloria became violently ill. Attempting to strangle her little girl, Gloria had to be restrained and ran off to the nearby banks of the Itaya where she tried to jump into the river and drown herself. Her mother quickly took her to her *compadre,* an *ayahuasquero* who lived in San Juan, a community a half hour's bus ride away. While under the effects of the purge, the healer saw Gloria's rival preparing an evil charm which she spread over a coin. Giving it to Gloria's husband, he in turn unknowingly passed the money on to Gloria for their child's support payment. The evil magic causing Gloria's illness was thus believed to be effected through this physical transference. Gloria visited the healer for almost a month, while he prescribed a series of herb baths which her mother carefully prepared. Within a couple of months,

things were back to normal. Gloria and her husband reconciled, but he never stopped seeing the other woman. Gloria said she did not feel completely cured and was planning to accompany me to visit her *ayahuasquero* again. I was very disappointed when this failed to materialize because the healer unexpectedly went off to Lima by plane. When I left Belén, Gloria had set up house with her husband at the edge of the community. Her husband would not permit her ever to return to her mother's house again. Maria, her mother, was a very knowledgeable woman in the realm of magic, although she was illiterate. Some even whispered that she was a witch. As a midwife, she delivered many babies in the community and was able to set broken bones and sprained joints. Maria had taken ayahuasca several times herself, and was a good apprentice. She knew many of the ayahuasca songs and boasted that her *compadre* would ask her to help sing them whenever she was able to attend a session. She often said that many of the good healers she knew had been killed by the envy of others.

José: An excellent hunter and fisherman, José supported his wife and ten children without any problems. There was always enough food in the house, and his handsome wife and he got on well, except for the constant squabbling that Ana would have with the neighbors. Full of anxiety, she would constantly become involved in neighborhood disputes, at times even going up to the police station to accuse one neighbor or other of theft, bewitchment, or the like. José's house was large and well built, and before he became ill, he was probably one of the more successful men in the community. He liked to drink, but within reasonable boundaries. One night, after he went out to bathe in the river at about 4:00 A.M. he received an electric shock from an eel. Taking to his bed, he got worse and worse, was unable to work, and began to excrete blood. At one point, his wife was sure he was going to die and considered leaving her children with her mother so that she could work for whatever sum she could earn to get money for food. They finally went to an *ayahuasquero* who lived in Belén. He had long ago cured Ana of a minor ailment and he was certain he could once again be of help. The healer first gave José a drink made from *toé* (a *datura* plant) mixed with cane alcohol, which seemed to operate as a tonic. José felt better immediately. The healer planned to give him ayahuasca, but his still weakened state made it necessary to wait until he became stronger. José was put on a special diet to prepare him for the purge, which had the effect of only weakening him. The lack of salt, sweets, and lard in his diet, and particularly the salt, made José very weak. Despite his earlier progress, he worsened very rapidly and took to his bed again. When I left Belén, José and Ana were planning to return to the healer to see who had caused the evil responsible for José's illness. His wife was certain that some envious neighbor who was jealous of José's many successes was the evildoer. In any case, the plan was that since José was still not strong enough to take the purge, his wife would do so and would report her visions to the healer. He would then be able to identify the source of the evil and deflect its power.

Teresa: A mother of five, this woman was living in an isolated jungle hamlet when she began to hemorrhage. A Catholic missionary group managed to send her by small plane to the city hospital in Iquitos and Teresa spent over a month and a half in the hospital. During this time, the bleeding was finally stopped by the medical personnel after some thirty days had passed. Their diagnoses of abdominal cancer was difficult to believe because of her good appetite and weight gain. Her children eventually brought her back to Belén to live with them in their balsa hut until she could recuperate. She went to see don Carlos, the healer mentioned earlier, who took her on as a patient. Her husband, Jaime, was sure that Teresa was suffering from *daño,* and in particular, vengeance from her former husband who no longer lived in Belén. Teresa had fought with him some eight years ago after which time they separated. The healer agreed that this ex-spouse was responsible for Teresa's illness and Carlos effected a cure. Prescribing herbs and medicines, he enabled her to undertake a long and arduous journey within a month's time, so that she could arrange some property that she had inherited from her parents.

Victor: Working as a day-laborer in the local lumber mill in Iquitos, Victor had a wooden house in the city suburb of Puchana. His salary didn't go very far, but his wife sold cooked food in a little stand near their home and they managed to get by. Victor spent a lot of time away from home, as did most of his friends, drinking beer and visiting *cantinas* (bars). Victor considered his life a peaceful one, but one day without warning, his wife packed her things and left him, taking along their seven-month-old child. Terribly upset and not knowing what to do, Victor was taken by one of his friends to an *ayahuasquero.* He was given the purge and had a vision in which his mother-in-law gave his wife a potion that made her become bored with him. At the next session he attended, Victor brought along an article of his wife's clothing so that the healer could use special songs and spells to make her return. Within a month's time she appeared at the door, and Victor took her in again without any explanation.

David: A middle-class migrant to Iquitos from the Peruvian coastal city of Trujillo, David was a sensitive young man of twenty-four interested in dance. He taught ballet at a local music school and studied art in his spare time at the regional Fine Arts school. When he began to have love problems, he became interested in ayahuasca. A young girl he liked very much and wanted to marry suddenly stopped seeing him because she became interested in another boy. David was sure that someone had caused him magical harm. He looked around for a healer whose reputation was known throughout the city and began to work with don Federico. As he attended several sessions and took the purge, David found that he was able to reconcile with his girl friend as a result of the healer's help. Moreover, as his body became used to the drug, he found that ayahuasca opened new avenues of perception for him in understanding the world of painting, which had been giving him some difficulties. It seemed to David that a new world of creativity was being opened by the continuing drug experiences and the insights into himself that he gained from it. When I left Iquitos, he was working as an apprentice with don Federico and continuing both his ballet teaching and painting.

Juana: Unlike most of the women whose interest in ayahuasca has been described, Juana was a fairly well-to-do woman of forty, married to an Iquitos restaurant owner. They both worked very hard at making a success of their business, which was a place for local intellectual activity. Paintings and sculpture adorned the premises and fine folkloric music from all of South America could be heard on their record player. A ready supply of regional dishes and jungle liquors made the restaurant an interesting place for evening entertainment. One day, Juana told of her experience with an *ayahuasquero*. She had developed a skin ailment which responded poorly to the pharmaceutical medicine prescribed by a town doctor. No one seemed able to help her. She finally visited an *ayahuasquero* and took the purge. While under the effects of the drug, she saw her mother-in-law (with whom she got on badly) prepare a concoction and slip it to her in a meal, causing her to become ill. She only visited the healer once. He gave her a salve to place cn the ailment, and told her he would neutralize the magic and make her better. The skin problem cleared up almost immediately and since that time she had no occasion to return to the healer.

## Some Comments

If we think about the men and women who are ayahuasca healers and patients, we see that they represent a cross-section of Iquitos, rich and poor, as Wils delineated in his sociological survey (1968). Few of the healers, however, in truth could be classified as *Cholos*. Although men such as don Antonio and don Carlos both live in Belén, the traditions which they inherit and share with others fit well within the admixture of Spanish beliefs and river-edge Indian therapeutic practices. The other two healers, don José and don Federico, are both well-established in Iquitos, and their life styles are quite similar to those of other men and women of middle income and mien. Ayahuasca healing in no way appears to be a simple retention of past Indian belief systems. The role of Spanish medieval beliefs as they became syncretized or blended with traditional ones, is important to keep in mind. The so-called "transistor revolution", where mass media finds its way into every tiny jungle niche, too, brings modern medicine's vocabulary to the tongues of many. It is not at all unusual for an *ayahuasquero* to talk of microbes, science, infections, tumors, lymph glands, and the like. Nonetheless, as must be repeatedly stressed, healing takes place well within the nexus of a philosophy of causation that sets up priorities in determining the magical origin of illness before any cure can be effected.

The healer's patients, too, share different social realities between them. Yet, as the biographies show, no one social segment to the exclusion of another overwhelms the healer's session, nor does there seem to be any difference in the number of men as contrasted to women who seek the help of the healer. Although Rios Reategui's study of actual patients in therapy will, when it appears, document the relative proportions of patients with regard to class membership, I might venture an educated guess that middle-income men and women, after trying alternative medical facilities, come to the healer's door in lesser numbers than the urban poor.

Perhaps I ought to add a word here about some of the difficulties that are presented to the social scientist who studies a quasi-legal area of esoteric beliefs. Certainly, the problem of sampling is important to consider. Dr. Seguín in Lima asked me prior to my field work in the rain forest how I would get to meet ayahuasca healers and what assurance I had that they would talk to me. Indeed, I explored every possible lead in order to find ayahuasca healers who would allow an interview and permit me to attend their sessions. Being a woman, I think, made it easier, especially since this was a society whose division of labor stresses particular activities for each sex. Most ayahuasca healers are men who might find another man presents a problem in terms of rivalry—possible envy of or malice toward their curing abilities. A woman, however, rarely seems to present such a threat, especially if she is a stranger to boot. On several occasions when I visited healers whom I had recently met, either alone or in the company of a patient, my reception was generally pleasant and the discussion quite open. However, on one occasion when I brought along my colleague to the slum to introduce him to a healer, the *ayahuasquero* literally hid in fear. He later told me he thought the visit was only a ruse to entrap and jail him. On another occasion, I was told by my informant that I could attend a drug session that night, but that I was not to bring my doctor friend along.

I think that possibly some of the problems in this area stemmed from the use of a medical as opposed to anthropological type of interview. In the first month or so of my study, I quickly learned that I couldn't use a barrage of direct questions. One of the first women I interviewed called me to my face a *"preguntona,"* or literally one who asks too many questions. In subsequent interviews with healers, I would make a point to speak of my interest in ayahuasca and how little we knew of the plant in my own country, and then patiently wait for the healer to talk about what he wanted to discuss. Actually, this turned out to be a wise procedure, especially since those first months when my colleague interviewed Juana in our balsa house. Earlier, she had described symptoms of a magical illness to me and I asked Dr. Rios to interview her. He questioned her concerning her symptoms, and she was subjected to a standard medical procedure that one might expect from visiting a doctor in a busy clinic or hospital. Later, however, Juana in no uncertain terms made it very clear that she was upset by the interview, and indeed related how the questions made her tremble. This was a good example to me of how not to procede in the future.

Interestingly enough, in a slum like Belén I found myself friendly with people who were neighbors but did not know one another. In fact, when I took up residence and began to receive visitors with greater frequency, I would often have to introduce people although they lived just a few streets away. These same men and women, however, on different occasions described details of their own ayahuasca treatment or else their expectations about the drug's effect. I was struck by the similarities of their visual experiences.

To cross-check some of this data, I paid particular attention to my card-reading data. I noticed my clients' interpretations of occurring misfortune cards in line with illness syndromes that I had learned about elsewhere. In this way, I was able to verify what I had learned concerning ayahuasca with another group of people whose contact with me had nothing directly to do with the plant's use. Although most of the people who came to me to have their fortunes read were often strangers and thus constituted what might be considered a random sample, there is probably some bias in favor of those who believed in luck.

When I returned to the United States and had occasion to read Karsten's account of the use of ayahuasca among the Jivaro (published in 1923 and based on research done years prior to that date), I found data on the guardian spirit of the vine which sounded as though it had come directly from the mouth of don Federico in Iquitos. If I were to argue for the persistence of traditional belief systems concerning ayahuasca, this is the best evidence I can offer. The Jivaro, living in the eastern part of the Ecuadorian rain forest, are separated by great distances from the urban healer I was quoting. Yet, despite the difference in time and space, similar belief systems had been independently reported by myself and another anthropologist. Moreover, one man such as don Federico, if willing to confide his system of ayahuasca healing, is more than an adequate source of esoteric beliefs, given his many years of healing practice and numerous clientele. At the end of the year, in retrospect, I was very pleased that through serendipity, I got to know men such as don Federico, who were kind and helpful in teaching me about the visionary vine.

In the next chapter, the content of ayahuasca visions will be examined from reports given to me by the people of Belén. It is interesting to observe the similarities of visions as they are culturally structured.

# Ayahuasca Visions

8

In the year that I worked in Belén, I spoke to many people about ayahuasca and its effects. Listening to scores of informants talk about their experience while taking the hallucinogen was very informative; but, after a couple of months, this became somewhat repetitious. The same kinds of visions kept occurring time after time, as former patients would describe jungle creatures such as boa constrictors and viperous snakes that appeared before them under ayahuasca. For the most part, after a certain confidence had been established among informants, details of illnesses suffered and their magical origin would be related as the reason for seeking a healer's help. Under the effects of the drug, a screen full of visions would appear to the person, often much more exciting than the occasional movie he might attend in the city. Although some claimed not to have received any visions under their particular ayahuasca experience, most did have things to relate. Both river and jungle animals would fill the mind's eye. Many people would claim to see the person or persons who were responsible for bewitching them. Some would report a panorama of activity, in which a person would express his innermost thoughts toward the patient, such as sexual desire, vengeance or hate, and then proceed to manufacture some medicine to throw over their threshold or perhaps slip unnoticed into a drink. Sometimes symbols would be reported, rather than panoramic action. One woman spoke of a church and a white veil that she saw in a sort of staccato vision, which represented to her how a rejected suitor wanted her to leave her husband and children to run off and get married. At times, a person would report seeing someone sneak up to their house at night to slip an evil potion across the threshold. At other times, someone might appear in a vision laughing sardonically at the man or woman whom they were causing to be bewitched. In other cases, a totally unknown man or woman would appear before a person in an ayahuasca vision. However, in all cases it was the job of the experienced *ayahuasquero* to interpret his patients' visions so as to clarify the cause of their illness. Quite often, people would say that their healer, while under the effects of the drug, would tell them he saw the person responsible for their misfortune, but would not say who it was. It was left for their own drug experience to bring forth this information. Through this kind of suggestion, the patient would be brought to a pitch of expectation. It is not difficult to imagine how affective need would be expressed by a particular vision or illusion stimulated by the drug.

When an unknown person appears before a patient, it becomes the healer's job to decide his identity. Many people, however, see members of their family or else people with whom they may be having personal difficulties appear before them, including neighbors, ex-spouses, in-laws, a rejected lover, and so on. If only part of a person is seen in profile, or a turned back or shoulder view, the healer once again is called upon to interpret this vision. The type of vision that is reported by a person may at times depend upon the rhythm of the songs the healer sings. A stacatto beat may bring forth many fleeting momentary visions, while slower songs may be used for more prolonged visionary experiences, such as the ones used to identify evildoers.

The many visions of snakes and boas reported by patients are used by healers to effect cures. It is widely believed that a snake (called in Spanish, *culebra*) is the mother spirit of the drug. Many herbs and medicines found in nature are believed to have protective spirits which watch over their plant's use and are jealous guardians. Such spirits on occasion must be propitiated when their plant is cut down or removed by man from the jungle confines. Some fishermen and hunters in Belén who regularly bring psychedelics back from the heart of the jungle to supply some of the ayahuasca healers in Iquitos leave offerings of tobacco and food under the tree when they cut off the woody vine. People often talk about the spirits of these plants as jealous guardians who must be given special attention. Ayahuasca is no exception here, and dietary prescriptions stressed again and again are justified by the jealous nature of the plant. It is for this reason that salt, sweets, and lard must be avoided by ayahuasca users for at least a twenty-four hour period preceding and following the use of the purge. At times, sexual abstinence may also be requested by the healer.

The mother spirit of ayahuasca may transform herself into an animate creature such as a princess, a queen, or any one of many different fantasy

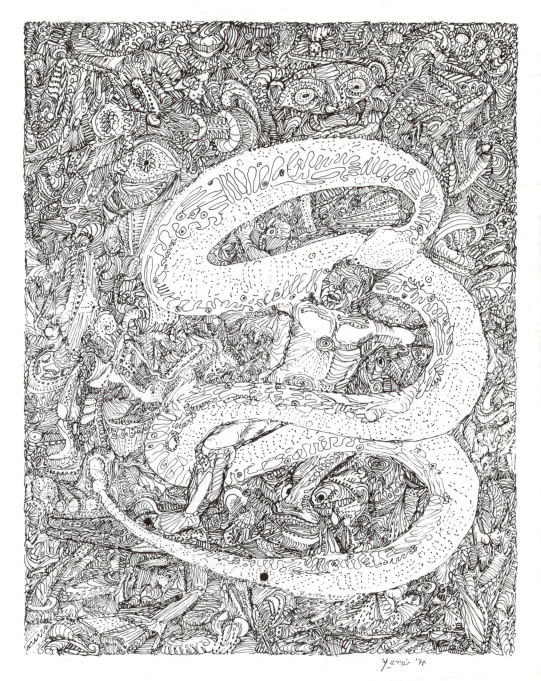

forms. This is done to find out if the person who takes the purge is strong or fearful. Strength is generally thought of in terms of self-domination, of not losing control of oneself under the effects of ayahuasca, nor screaming in fear as jungle creatures fill one's visions. For example, a commonly reported vision is that a very large snake enters the circle around which a person is seated in the jungle or else enters a room where one is taking ayahuasca. If the patient is not frightened by this creature, the snake begins to teach the person his song. In a good session, a certain moment will arrive when everyone who is under the effects of the drug begins to sing a series of songs at the same time as they are visited by the snake in their visions. A frightening vision is often described in which a boa enters the patient's mouth. Often identified as the *Yacumama* of folklore, these boa constrictors in everyday jungle life are enough to cause horror to the most stout-hearted person. Although poisonless, such a creature measures over twenty-five feet long and one foot wide. Its force is prodigious, and people say it can eat animals of great size. If a person is able to remain cool and not panic, this is a sign that he will be cured. As the boa enters one's body, it is a further omen to the man or woman with such expectations that he will be protected by the ayahuasca spirit. As with don Federico, many healers prepare their patients for the drug experience by discussing such common visions. Expectation among the *Cholos,* at least, is great that such snakes will appear before them.

In the West, when we read reports of hallucinogenic drug experiences (see, for example, Ebin, 1961), we don't generally find similar kinds of visionary experience reported as we do in the rain forest. Cultural expectations connected with the use of a hallucinogen such as ayahuasca must be seen as the explanation for the recurrence of the similarity in types of visions. Although I spoke to many people who had never taken ayahuasca, most adults would comment in great detail about points of information concerning the vine, which could later be verified with healers or former patients. The presence of beliefs and expectations of these people vis-á-vis the drug's action must be seen as influencing the similarities reported in the actual drug experience.

This occurs not only among the urban poor, but with primitive use of ayahuasca as well. One recent study of the use of the psychedelic vine among the Cashinahua Indians of Peru by Kensinger (1970), found a certain frequency of occurrence and a high degree of similarity in the content of particular hallucinations. Kensinger's informants reported brightly colored large snakes, jaguars, and ocelots, spirits of ayahuasca, large trees often falling, lakes often filled with anacondas and alligators, traders and their goods, and gardens. All quite frequently were reported with a sense of motion. Certainly, other factors of interest to most drug researchers enter the picture here, such as the personality and past experience of the person taking the substance, the setting in which the drug is taken, the dosage level and so on. However, cultural variables must be stressed once again as a primary aspect of drug use. When reports made my Europeans and Americans who have taken ayahuasca are compared to jungle populations, some interesting contrasts emerge. The following are some brief descriptions of experiences under ayahuasca that Westerners, lacking a cultural tradition of drug use have described for ayahuasca or its alkaloids. My own experience with the vine has been included in these accounts.

Richard Spruce: A British botanist from Yorkshire, Spruce traveled throughout the Amazon and its tributaries from 1849 to 1864. He made extensive collections of South American flora and was the first modern investigator to identify ayahuasca in 1851, although his materials were published posthumously. Actually, the geographer Villavicencio wrote of the vine in his *Geography of Ecuador,* which appeared in 1858. Spruce observed the used of the liana among the Tukanoan tribes of the Uaupes River in the Brazilian Amazon. He wrote of the caapi-drinking ceremony as follows:

I had gone with the full intention of experimenting the caapi myself, but I had scarcely dispatched one cup of the nauseous beverage, which is but half the dose, when the ruler of the feast . . . came up with a woman bearing a large calabash of *caxiri* (mandioca beer), of which I must needs take a copious draught, and as I know the mode of its preparation, it was gulped down with secret loathing. Scarcely had I accomplished this feat, when a large cigar 2 feet long and as thick as the wrist was put lighted into my hand, and etiquette demanded that I should take a few whiffs of it—I who had never in my life smoked a cigar or a pipe of tobacco. Above all this, I must drink a large cup of palm wine, and it will readily be understood that the effect of such a complex dose was a strong inclination to vomit, which was only overcome by lying down in a hammock and drinking a cup of coffee. (Cited in Schultes 1970, p. 26).

We can see from the above that Spruce did not describe very many details of his own experience, except of course, some interesting side comments on his disgust with native alcoholic intoxicants.

Michael J. Harner: An American anthropologist trained at the University of California at Berkeley, Dr. Harner is now a professor of anthropology at the New School for Social Research in New York. He went to study the Jivaro Indians of the Ecuadorian Amazon in 1956–1957. During the first year that Dr. Harner worked among the Jivaro, he didn't appreciate the psychological impact of the *natema* or ayahuasca drink upon the native view of reality. The drink itself has many names in different parts of the Amazon—called *yagé* or *yajé* in Colombia, ayahuasca in Peru and parts of Ecuador, and *caapi* in Brazil. The Jivaro are among the best known Amazonian group to use this preparation in crossing over to the supernatural world at will to deal with the forces they believe influence and even determine the events of waking life. In 1961 Dr. Harner returned to the Ecuadorian Amazon and was able to drink the hallucinogenic brew in the course of fieldwork with another Upper Amazon Basin tribe.

For several hours after drinking the brew, Harner found himself, although awake, in a world literally beyond his wildest dreams. He met bird-headed people as well as dragon-like creatures who explained that they were the true gods of this world. He enlisted the services of other spirit helpers in attempting to fly through the far reaches of the Galaxy. He found himself transported into a trance where the supernatural seemed natural and realized that anthropologists, including himself, had profoundly underestimated the importance of the drug in affecting native ideology. In 1964, Dr. Harner returned to the Jivaro and studied the shamanistic use of the plant. An article he published in 1968 in *Natural History* reproduces drawings of one Jivaro shaman, who drew figures of what he saw while under the influence of the powerful *natema*. Snakes, devils of the Christian religion and jaguars were some of the things he saw (1968: 28ff).

Chilean Psychiatric Patients: The Chilean psychiatrist, Claudio Naranjo, administered one of the three major alkaloids of ayahuasca, called harmaline, to a population of thirty volunteers in Santiago under controlled conditions. The reactions of these persons are interesting to examine. Physical sensations accompanied the drug experience, with a sense of numbness of the hands or feet generally present. Distortions of body image were only rarely encountered, while subjects indicated isolated physical symptoms such as pressure in the head, discomfort in the chest or enhancement of sensations such as breathing or blinking. Eighteen of the volunteers reported dizziness or general malaise, which tended to appear or disappear throughout the session. As far as perception was concerned, rarely were distortions of forms, alterations in the sense of depth or changes in the expression of faces part of the drug's effect. Naranjo found that with harmaline, the environment remains essentially unchanged, both in regard to its formal and aesthetic qualities. With eyes open, the most often reported phenomenon was the superposition of images on surfaces such as walls or ceiling. Or else imaginary scenes would be viewed simultaneously along with an undistorted perception of surrounding objects. Such imagery, however, was not usually taken to be "reality." Some people described lightning-like flashes.

When the subject's eyes were closed, colors were predominantly red-green or blue-orange contrasts. Among his middle-class urban Chilean volunteers, Naranjo reported the occurrence of certain themes such as felines, Negroes, and flying. More than half the subjects reported buzzing sounds in their heads. When he gave his patients mescaline at a later date and compared the two sets of reports, he found that harmaline effected emotional activity less than mescaline. Thinking, too, was affected only in subtle ways, if at all. Naranjo found

his patients concerned with religious or philosophical problems under harmaline's effects. The typical reaction could be said to be a closed-eye contem-
plation of vivid imagery without further effect than wonder and interest in its
significance. The psychiatrist concluded that this was quite in contrast to the
ecstatic heavens or dreadful hells of other hallucinogens. Interestingly enough,
although harmaline had a lesser effect on the intensity of feelings, it did cause
qualitative changes in emotions. In Naranjo's opinion, this may have accounted for the pronounced amelioration of neurotic symptoms which eight
of the thirty subjects evidenced.

Desire to communicate was found to be slight under the effects of harmaline. Other persons were felt to be part of the external world and such contact
was avoided. Some of Naranjo's subjects felt that certain scenes which they saw
had really happened, with their own disembodied presence bearing witness to
them in a different time and place. He saw this to match the experience
reported for South American shamans who take ayahuasca for purposes of
divination. In further animal experimentations Naranjo did with harmaline,
he found complex brain modification which permitted him to conclude that
the neurophysiological picture matches that of the traditional ayahuasca
dreaming often reported, in that the states he described involved lethargy,
immobility, closed eyes and generalized withdrawal from the environment. At
the same time there was an alertness to mental processes and an activation of
fantasy (Naranjo, 1967: 385).

Allen Ginsberg: The well-known poet Allen Ginsberg and the writer William S. Burroughs corresponded about the powerful psychedelic vine. Burroughs' early letters to Ginsberg in 1951 described his picaresque search for
the mind-expanding drug, known in Colombia as *yagé*. Some seven years later,
Ginsberg wrote to Burroughs about his own experience with ayahuasca in
Pucallpa, Peru. Excerpts from the following letter published in *Yagé Letters*,
is dated June 10, 1960:

> . . . the first time, much stronger than the drink I had in Lima, Ayahuasca, can
> be bottled and transported and stay strong, as long as it does not ferment—needs
> well closed bottle. Drank a cup—slightly fermented also—lay back and after an
> hour . . . began seeing or feeling what I thought was the Great Being, or some sense
> of It, approaching my mind like a big wet vagina—lay back in that for a while—
> only image I can come up with is of a big black hole of God—Nose thru which I
> peered into a mystery—and the black hole surrounded by all creation particularly
> colored snakes—all real.
> I felt somewhat like what this image represents, the sense of it so real.
> The eye is imaginary image, to give life to the picture. Also a great feeling of
> pleasantness in my body, no nausea. Lasted in different phases about 2 hours—the
> effects wore off after 3—the phantasy itself lasted from ¾ of hour after I drink to
> 2½ hours later more or less (Burroughs, 1963: 51).

Ginsberg also describes a second experience as follows:

. . . then lay down expecting God knows what other pleasant vision and then I began to get high—and then the whole fucking Cosmos broke loose around me, I think the strongest and worst I've ever had it nearly (I still reserve the Harlem experiences, being Natural, in abeyance. The LSD was Perfection but didn't get me so deep in nor so horribly in)—First I began to realize my worry about the mosquitoes or vomiting was silly as there was the great stake of life and Death—I felt faced by Death, my skull in my beard on pallet and porch rolling back and forth and settling finally as if in reproduction of the last physical move I make before settling into real death—got nauseous, rushed out and began vomiting, all covered with snakes, like a Snake Seraph, colored serpents in aureole all around my body, I felt like a snake vomiting out the universe . . . (p. 51–52).

Ginsberg's visions continued with spectral rays around the hut in which he was taking ayahuasca. Although the crooning of the *maestro* was comforting, he was frightened and lay there with waves of fear rolling over him. He resigned himself to whatever fate was in store, after a thorough examination of his soul. He feared he would go mad, he wrote, if he took *yagé* again, although he had plans to go upriver on a six-hour journey to take ayahuasca again with an Indian group.

Richard Evans Schultes: An eminent American botanist and world authority on narcotic and stimulating plants, Dr. Schultes is now director of the Harvard Botanical Museum. He spent fourteen years from 1941 to 1954 living with various Indian groups of the South American Amazon, and has identified many little-known hallucinogenic plants. He became interested in Spruce's work on South America and retraced most of his itinerary, re-collecting many of the plants that Spruce originally found in that area. Schultes' list of publications is enormous: he has worked in areas from Mexico to Brazil. Editor of the prestigious journal, *Economic Botany,* Dr. Schultes has spent much of his botanical career in helping to clarify taxonomic problems connected with the ayahuasca vine. Like other scientists in the field of botany, psychiatry and medicine, Schultes prefers not to take anyone's word that a particular plant can cause a particular effect. Whenever possible, he has taken preparations in ritual settings along with his informants.

In discussing his own *Banisteriopsis* experience, he mentions that it is often difficult to describe an ayahuasca intoxication since the effects of the alkaloid harmine, apparently the prime psychoactive agent, does react variably from one person to another. Moreover, methods of preparing the plant differ from area to area and admixtures can alter the effects of the drink's principal ingredient.

Dr. Schultes summarizes his own experiences as follows: ". . . The intoxication began with a feeling of giddiness and nervousness, soon followed by nausea, occasional vomiting and profuse perspiration. Occasionally, the vision was disturbed by flashes of light and upon closing the eyes, a bluish haze sometimes appeared. A period of abnormal lassitude then set in during which colors increased in intensity. Sooner or later a deep sleep interrupted by dream-like sequence began. The only after-effect noticed was intestinal upset and diarrhea on the following day" (1970: 28).

Marlene Dobkin de Rios: When I spent three months in 1967 studying mescaline healing in the Peruvian coast, I observed several ritual sessions where I was invited to drink the hallucinogenic potion. Yet, although it was readily available to me, I must admit that I was frightened, in fact horrified to imagine all the terrible things that self-knowledge might bring me. Sure as I was that I was harboring all sorts of incurable neuroses within, I hesitated and decided not to try the San Pedro brew. Many rationalizations sprung to mind—time was short and I might have bad side-effects. What would I do if the after effects were so severe that I couldn't continue my work? I felt alone, and what would happen if my self-protective shield was knocked over? And so, despite the kindly offers of my informants and the healers I visited, I resolved not to try the mescaline cactus.

When I returned home and wrote up my field experiences about San Pedro use, it seemed as though I had somehow missed the point. In October 1967, I was invited to participate in a conference sponsored by the R. Bucke Society in Montreal, Canada. Bucke was a Canadian psychiatrist who coined the term cosmic consciousness. The society which bore his name was concerned with religious and mystical states in which Bucke showed much interest, despite the general disdain and scorn such matters still hold for many serious scientists. At the meeting, after listening to various participants discuss some aspect of the question, "Do Psychedelic Drugs have Religious Significance?" (see Prince, 1969), I realized that the reality I reported on was quite a different one than that of people who used such substances for mystical or religious purposes. By the time I returned to Peru in June of 1968 to begin my ayahuasca study, I sensed that if I were ever to go beyond the detachment that I had so carefully cultivated, I would have to take ayahuasca myself.

Yet, as the months passed and opportunities presented themselves to try ayahuasca, I still managed to avoid the experience. Finally, the time approached for me to leave Iquitos to participate in a symposium on "Hallucinogens and Shamanism," which was to be held at the American Anthropological Association's annual meeting in Seattle, Washington. I knew that I would be addressing a large group of my colleagues about a substance which in truth, I had to admit I knew very little. Although I had been collecting data for almost five months on ayahuasca, it was really just hearsay evidence. I often had the smug feeling that I was the only sane person in an insane world. Resolved then finally to take the purge, I decided first to take advantage of the availability of a small dose of 100 micrograms of LSD, which my colleague and I originally planned to give to the healers we worked with at the end of our study. Unfortunately, this plan did not materialize, as legal production of such substances was terminated. Nonetheless, I was able to take the LSD at home under medical supervision, albeit in the comfort of my Iquitos house, surrounded by the music I liked, with a friend as company and in the presence of paintings, folk art, and flowers. Two weeks later I took an unknown dose of ayahuasca mixed with *chacruna* (probably containing DMT) under the supervision of don Antonio. My experience with LSD was simply one of the most aesthetically rewarding experiences I have ever had in my life. Accompanied by eighteenth century harp music which seemed endless in its reception, I could not really describe the aesthetic dimensions of the fast-moving kaleideoscopic visions, although many medieval images probably invoked by the quality of the music filled my vision. As the height of these pseudo-illusions lessened, I found myself discussing who I was, what I was doing, what I wanted from life, what life meant to me, and a series of questions that I hadn't been concerned with since I was a teenager. I might point out that at the beginning of the session, upon the advice of a friend, I decided to *ponerme en blanco*—or simply, to flow with the force of the experience. From my readings about drug experiments, I knew that a common feature of the "bad trip" was the resistence that a person might offer in attempting to hold back or try to control the drug's effects.

When I took ayahuasca, the previous LSD experience stood me in good stead in that my book-learned expectations had been replaced by the real thing. It was with enthusiastic expectation that I met don Antonio one Monday night, along with my colleague, to take the ayahuasca brew that had been prepared for me.

That evening in Belén, Antonio was even busier than usual, attending to the many patients who came to him to be exorcised or treated for assorted ailments. I sat patiently for over an hour, chatting with my colleague, Dr. Rios, who had just returned from a brief trip to Lima. He was full of details about the people we knew. Finally, Antonio led us through a maze of houses to a distant reach of Venecia, where a friend of his allowed him to use his floating balsa house for our session. Two other people were present, but I paid very little attention to them in my nervousness.

We got comfortably seated on the floor of the house, and Antonio passed the potion around. I noticed as I drank that Antonio, to be sure that the "gringa" got her full share of visions, gave me a cup brim-full of the not so pleasant-smelling liquid. Others who drank that night, in retrospect, seemed to have been given a much smaller amount.

The following is an account of what happened.

About ten minutes later, feelings of strangeness came over my body and I had difficulty in coordinating extremities. Quick-arriving visual forms and movements flit before my eyes some twenty minutes after taking the drink, and a certain amount of anxiety that was not difficult to handle was felt, especially when Halloween-type demons in primary reds, greens and blues loomed large and then receded before me. Very fast-moving imagery almost like Bosch's paintings appeared, which at times were difficult to focus upon. At one point after I touched the arm of my friend for reassurance, the primary colors changed to flaming yellows and pinks, as a cornucopia full of warmth filled the visions before my eyes and gave me a sort of peripheral vision extending toward the person I had touched. Then in harmony with the healer's *schacapa*, a series of leaf-faced visions appeared, while my eyes remained open. They were followed by a full-length colored vision of a Peruvian woman, unknown to me but sneering in my direction, which appeared before me. Then more visions arrived, followed by heavy vomiting and diarrhea which lasted for about three hours.

In New York, where I grew up, vomiting was hardly anything to celebrate, and I remember my concern at the terrible noises I made with the "dry heaves" that afflicted me. Yet, later on, when chatting with others, I realized that in the rain forest, people periodically induced vomiting in their children so as to purge them of the various parasitical illnesses which are rampant in the region. My colleague told me later on that don Antonio in his subsequent healing sessions would often refer to the gringa who had voimited heavily with aya-huasca and the terrible noises she made. He even imitated me to the great amusement of his audience.

Throughout the experience, any light was painful to my eyes. Time was experienced as very slow-moving. After-effects included physical weakness for a day or two, but a general sense of well-being and looseness in dealing with others.

At this point, it might be interesting to examine some of my experiences under ayahuasca, since my own lack of a cultural expectation toward the use of such a substance gave me differing responses than those reported by the informants with whom I worked, despite the fact that I had been collecting data on informants' visions. No jungle creatures filled my vision, nor did I experience the often-reported floating sensation. The visions I had contained symbols of my own culture. The unknown woman who appeared to me in my vision was dressed very much like the urban poor among whom I worked, but she somehow looked more opulent and well-off than many of the near-starving friends I had made in Belén. I remember my curiosity at her apparent dislike of me and that she should behave in that manner, but I didn't pay much attention to the vision nor did it change my mood at all. Later on, when telling of my experiences to friends in Belén, some ventured that this woman who appeared to me may have been responsible for a parasitic illness I developed during the course of my work. I could see how people appearing before a sick person might easily be linked to malice regardless of whether or not they are known to the patient. Had I grown up in this society and received continual conditioning toward a belief in magical source of sickness, it is quite probable that I would have interpreted this vision as a revelation of who it was that caused me to become ill.

When I took ayahuasca, I was unaware of the unwritten rule about not touching another person. I was later told by the healer who guided my ayahuasca session that I had received a double dose of the potion by touching another person and magically had the experience of two doses. The vomitting and diarrhea that afflicted me, thus, were my own fault for not following precepts that were unknown to me. The Peruvian painter, Yando, whose arm I touched during the session has prepared a series of drawings portraying the visions he has had under the influence of ayahuasca. In addition, he has made some ink drawings of the sessions, (see p. 70) which are difficult to photograph because of the problem of pupilary dilation and painful light. That evening, he had no visions from the purge.

The feelings of well-being that dodged my steps for several months after the ayahuasca experience were one area, however, that did overlap with my informants reports. Many people agree that the ayahuasca experience stays with them for a long time, relaxing them and making their dealings with others somewhat more easy and fruitful.

# Mechanisms
of Healing

Throughout the history of medicine we find that many cures have been effective despite the irrational concepts of disease that members of a society might hold. To the Western observer it might appear in fact that ayahuasca use is totally irrational in terms of the magical world view in which such healing occurs. After all, how can "spirits" of inanimate nature or the malice of people possibly make one ill, when microbes, viruses, organic malfunctions, and the like are the true offenders? Yet, to the Amazonian man or woman whose beliefs are thus oriented, ayahuasca can only be viewed as a valuable adjunct in reaffirming one's own suspicions about illness and its etiology. Once the premises concerning the philosophy of causation are accepted, the system of healing itself has an inner rationale that is quite in accordance with a richly developed historical tradition.

### Healing Techniques

The use of ayahuasca to heal does not include a well-defined sense of the hallucinogen as a curative agent, *per se*. Rather, the vine is seen to operate as a powerful means to a desired end—it gives the healer entry into the culturally important area of disease causality, enabling him to identify the nature of the illness from which a person is suffering, and then to deflect or neutralize the evil magic which is deemed responsible for illness. When we examine the successes attributed

129

to the healer, we fine that in general terms a selection process is at work in which healers accept patients whom they feel they will have a good chance of reaching. Simple illnesses are rarely treated with the drug, but herbs, plants, and store-bought medicines are prescribed by the healer for these types of affliction. Nor are psychotic patients given ayahuasca.

Needless to say, drug healers do not accept all patients who come to them for help, nor are they able to cure everyone with an infusion of ayahuasca. But many of the patients who do find their way to the jungle sessions are precisely those whose anxieties, fears, projections of hostility and hatred toward others would in Western medicine be grist for psychiatric help. Drug healing in the Peruvian jungle in many ways represents a very old and honored tradition of dealing with psychological problems that predates Freudian analysis by centuries.

In addition to the use of the powerful vine, a healer will practice time-honored curing traditions, including whistling, singing, praying, and reciting orations, called *icaros,* which are believed to be preventative, to assure a patient that no evil will befall him from a friend's betrayal or a spouse's scorn. Acting as counters to evil magic, *icaros* may be used for diverse ends. A healer may also suck at afflicted regions of the body to extract thistles that have been magically placed there to cause illness, or else blow *mapacho* cigarette smoke over the body of the patient.

*Ayahuasqueros* often make an immediate diagnosis by taking a patient's pulse without the use of a clock or watch. They say that such activity tells them what type of illness the sick man or woman is suffering from and may be one way to determine the presence of deep anxiety stemming from belief in witchcraft. Healers often prescribe a drink of cane alcohol mixed with camphor, which acts to "pep-up" or stimulate and is often prescribed in daily dosages. It is a cerebral excitant (Lewin, 1964: 145) and can produce some mild euphoria. In addition, *ayahuasqueros* use varied techniques such as reassurance, important in many cases, to offer at least temporary help. On the negative side of the ledger, depending on the degree of anxiety, this kind of reassurance must be constantly repeated to be effective (Weiss and English, 1956: 12). Suggestion and persuasion are also of great importance in order to convince a patient that the healer's advice is good and that benefits will accrue to him, should he follow his advice (*Ibid.*: 154).

To return to an earlier point, ayahuasca is not the only hallucinogenic substance used in healing. Other plants such as a leaf called *chacruna* (*B. rusbyana,* believed to contain N-N-dimethyltryptamine) may be added to the preparation to increase the effects. Others may use a substance called *toé* (*Datura suavoleons),* which by itself is strong enough to alter states of consciousness. Not very much is known at present about the effects of mixing together various hallucinogenic substances, but different healers in the rain forest prefer those mixtures they know best from their apprenticeship days. At times a tobacco that has hallucinogenic effects and feelings of *mareacíon* (dizziness) and probably containing *Nicotiana tabacum* may be used by a healer for particular cases. This latter substance grown in the rain forest is several times stronger in effect than similar species grown in North America (see Janiger and Dobkin de Rios, n.d.).

## Ayahuasca and the Non-Verbal

Very much a part of healing techniques is the use to which special songs or whistling incantations are put. Although some recent psychological studies of drug therapy have focused upon the importance of the non-verbal (see in particular Eisner, 1966), many drug-adjuncted therapeutic sessions in Western society are closely directed situations in which talking plays a most important role. Yet, as Eisner argues, during the most crucial moments of life words often interfere with the main flow of communication. In fact, much of the therapeutic interaction can and does take place at the non-verbal level (*Ibid.:* 542). While verbal performance in Western society may be highly valued and rewarded, Peruvian rain forest residents are much less geared to verbal excesses. During many of the ayahuasca sessions, for example, patients are left to themselves to experience the effects of the drug with little if any verbal prodding on the part of the healer. Caldwell (1968) points at the similarity in some European clinics today where hallucinogens are incorporated into psychotherapy. When music is part of the drug experience, it is probable that the experience, per se, is a more integrative one. Music may actually potentiate the drug experience, removing it from the realm of the intellectual and into the area of pure feelings. Music, of course, can also help to manipulate mood. Both modern and traditional healers who use such auditory aids in many ways enrich the experience by presenting stimuli that can enter all channels of a person's perception. The use of perfumed water *(agua florida),* which is drunk by the patient during the ayahuasca session, is no doubt another way in which non-verbal olfactory aspects are capitalized upon.

## Comments

Ayahuasca music is utilized only in drug ceremonies, and contrasts musicologically to the considerable corpus of music which falls within a secular category. This latter group comprises music played on happy occasions, such as religious festivals within the Roman Catholic Church, and melodies played during wakes. On the latter occasions, friends and relatives accompany the body of the deceased throughout an evening to dawn vigil. Such melodies are generally played with a drum *(tambor)*, *quena* (wooden reedless flute found in the Andean highlands), and a four-string violin, probably of Spanish origin.

It is tempting to suggest a comparison between ayahuasca whistling incantations and such music as the Gregorian chants, at least insofar as basic function goes. Just as one can argue that Gregorian chants and ecclesiastical modes represent tonal relationships in which scales are structured so as to evoke a spiritual experience within the context of Christianity, so too might the ayahuasca music be viewed as an essential component of a non-ordinary reality sustained by the sensory overload inherent in drug-induced alteration in consciousness. Such music, of course, cannot be divorced from its social context. We should reflect, for a moment, on the nature of hallucinogenic experience, per se, and the quality of reality alteration for the individual. Such phenomena as the slowing down or changing of time perception (see Ludwig, 1969: 14) must be related to how music is perceived by the individual under the effects of the powerful alkaloids present in the ayahuasca potion. The number of metronomic markings in a given piece of music may not, indeed, be perceived as they would be in an ordinary state. In fact, during my own experience under ayahuasca, some interesting aspects of the relationship of the music and the content of my visions could be determined. Fast-moving visions and detailed panorama of primary colors and variegated forms, difficult to focus on, could be correlated with my perception of the speed of the healer's music. When don Antonio slowed down his pace and a full-sized portrait of a woman appeared before me, I could, on later reflection, relate the vision's appearance to the slowing down of the healer's whistling incantations. Visions do change frequently from fast to slow, and seem to be controlled or evoked by the healer who is the creative force in deciding which melodies to call upon. When I was further into the drug experience and became nauseous and vomited, don Antonio reassured me that his continuing melodies would alleviate the nausea and cause it to pass away.

During ayahuasca sessions, both healer and patient take the drug together. Nonetheless, the healer is generally quite occupied in the performance of his ritual activities mentioned earlier and leaves his patients generally seated by themselves for major portions of the ceremony, only occasionally counseling or treating them directly. Healers state that certain melodies evoke certain types of visions. As I illustrated above, slower incantations may be responsible for the often-reported visions of men and women who are later identified as evil-doers. Perhaps, and one can only speculate here, faster incantations are crucial in the changeover from one reality to another. Such sensory overload has been frequently reported to produce anxiety in the individual, especially in initial drug-induced states. In Western society, LSD-like substances have been utilized in psychotherapy, often by Freudian-oriented analysts. Vomiting and nausea, which may occur in such cases, have occasionally been related to the inability of individuals to deal with anxiety generated by rapid access to unconscious realms. It may be that the role of such music as the whistling incantations during such anxiety states is to help carry the individual more easily into this second realm.

One additional facet of drug-induced experience that should be mentioned is the role that the guide or guru plays as an important other, toward whom the patient may turn in an anxious or highly suggestible state as the result of his alteration in consciousness. Masters and Houston (1966) discuss the vital place of the guru in guiding such sessions. It is possible that augmented suggestibility on the part of the patient encounters in the presence of the healer a creative source and origin of music which alleviates anxiety, tranquilizes, and causes a turning inward, by the musical evocation of particular visions.[1]

I might further speculate that fearful visions in an ayahuasca session could generally be attributed to the inadequate musical ability on the part of a particular healer.

### Placebo Effects of the Ayahuasca Potion

When people who believe they have been bewitched visit a healer, they are frequently given a potion of ayahuasca to help them see who it is that has caused their illness. As with other hallucinogenic drugs, a non-ordinary state of reality fills the hours of drug experience and is one that is unlike any other than most men or women have ever had.

The possibility suggests itself that the plant operates merely as a placebo —an inactive or inert drug given merely to produce a "satisfying" effect upon the patient. Is it possible that faith in the curative power of the drug itself is enough to cure? It think we have to dismiss this possibility, which may enter into a discussion of LSD therapy in the United States and Canada. There, insights into personal problems have often been examined by an analyst who guides the session.[2] Ayahuasca is not used to obtain verbal insight, and external rather than internal forces are viewed as responsible for disease. Man is, in effect, absolved from any responsibility. Especially in cases of *saladera* and situations involving interpersonal stress, the impact of such external forces is most clearly seen. Moreover, little of the biochemical effects of ayahuasca's healing properties are known. From my own personal experience, I would guess that strong hallucinogens like ayahuasca manage to relieve feelings of anxiety and tension which can build up to intolerable levels. Yet, although one

[1]See Katz (1971) for a transcription of an ayahuasca musical session and discussion.
[2]See Caldwell (1966), Abramson (1967)

would hesitate to call the purge a healing hallucinogen, it is possible that future evidence may point up more clearly the curative potential of the drug from a pharmacological point of view.

Nonetheless, both healer and patient are crucially concerned with identifying the nature of the illness, which in psychosomatic disorders may be very generalized pains and aches throughout the body. When people known to the patient or even total strangers appear in his visions, a skilled healer will attribute his patient's illness to such apparitions. Generalized, free-floating anxiety which immobilizes can then be changed into straightforward fear and placed squarely on the shoulders of the acknowledged evil person or spirit. A healer is especially successful in those cases when his patient believes him to be imnipotent and if an aura of personal success surrounds him. Thus, the healer may be able to relieve his patient's symptoms quickly and dramatically, when the patient believes the healer is powerful enough to counteract the evil magic directed against himself.

People rarely focus upon ayahuasca by itself as a curative agent. The hallucinogen is a means toward an end—a way in which healing can begin. Special diets, rituals, orations, particular spells, and counter magic are the ways in which healing takes place. Reassurance, suggestion, counseling as well as other techniques to be discussed shortly are all part of the cure, but the drug's role thoughtout is strongly diagnostic and revelatory.

### The Omnipotence of the Healer

Attempts are made by the healer to radiate total control and mastery over the unknown, especially in the realm of illness. Although he may turn to magical means in his healing procedures, nonetheless he employs very definite pragmatic means such as modern medicines, herb baths, and teas as well as a host of plants whose effects he has studied. The role of ayahuasca is connected to the aura of omnipotence surrounding the healer. Certainly the purge is a powerful persuader in its own right. Yet, given the belief system existing in the jungle, what seems to be most important to his patients is the healer's ability to deflect evil magic and neutralize its effect, or diagnose the sickness by means of the drug. Ayahuasca gives him entry into a world of magic by which he can effect his cures all that much more effectively. Even techniques such as his subtle reassurance, boasting in a generally non-boasting society, an all-knowing manner, subtle use of cues to let present and perspective patients know of his successes, his show of wealth, and his skills all enter into the picture. Two examples that illustrate healers' techniques come to mind here. In one case connected with doña Teresa mentioned earlier, after she had taken ayahuasca and her hemorrhage stopped, she was able to move about and take on some of her daily household chores. The next time her healer stopped by to see how she was doing, he stayed only a short while, as he had to visit another patient who was *really ill* (the healer's emphasis), and not nearly as well and thriving and about to recover as Teresa was. She repeated this conversation to several of her neighbors and family during the next few days and in fact did feel much better, no doubt in part because of this reassurance and support that the healer provided her.

In another case, I was present at a preliminary interview in which a healer chatted with two girls who had love problems and were looking for his help to try to capture their boyfriends' souls once and for all. Don Fernando, the healer, sat comfortably on a bench and talked about his many successes in healing. He boasted that in his home, an expensive fishing net costing well over $100 was sitting idle and rotting. Although he could make a good living at fishing, he was forced to give it up by the press of patients, he said, who came to him to be healed. Both girls were visibly impressed by his stated affluence and by his confident, assured manner, which indicated to them that he would and most definitely could help them in their love problems.

The myth of the omnipotence of some healers has become so strong that tales of ayahuasca millionaires have grown up and become repeated with some frequency. Both Iquitos and Pucallpa are known for at least one such aya-huasca millionaire—men who achieved fame in healing and who overnight built fine brick houses for themselves and their families. One famous healer in Pucallpa was imprisoned by the local police, finally to be released when a political demonstration followed in the wake of this incident. A spiritualist healer in Iquitos recounted the story of another colleague who had recently died. He had made his fortune in ayahuasca. Multiple property holdings and an affluent family attested to this healer's success with the purge.

Peruvian medical writers, much closer in time and space to folk healing than their American counterparts, are quite aware of its influence on large segments of their society and at times become threatened by the apparent successes and popularity of drug healers. Many such writers, in fact, have labeled both drug-adjuncted and popular folk healing charlatanism. One writer makes a fine distinction between highland healers who work within the confines of their Indian peasant community and the so-called charlatans of other regions. Tricking patients while under the effects of drug used in healing has been another accusation that has been leveled. These aspects of folk healing are difficult to dismiss lightly. Collective belief in the efficacy of the drug, the suggestibility engendered by such drug use and the skill of the healer who effects cures to patients often suffering from psychosomatic or psychoneurotic illness must be taken into account. Whether these cures are temporary remissions are not important here. The first-rate empirical knowledge of many healers concerning the rich pharmacopoeia available to them is undeniable.

The ability of the healer, whose skills are well-touted, his firm and confident manner in dealing with his patients, his boasts of the healing he has and will achieve—in short, the potency of the suggestive phenomena at work cannot be ignored. Certainly artifice is employed in the curer's art. One writer has maintained that "cultural symbols and values are the medium through which the individual patient approaches what is offered to him in a psychotherapy situation and that his response to the strategies of the therapist will be circumscribed by the meaning they have for him in terms of his general life view."[3] Healers do work within a belief system held by their patients and are able to manipulate the symbols shared by their patients in order to heal them that much more effectively.

For example, before allowing their patients to take the purge, many healers will undergo periods of up to a week of exorcising the evil believed to afflict such patients. This becomes a very necessary part of therapy because many people in this community operate in a confused social reality where magical beliefs function close to and at times in competition with scientific ones. The healer, in order to alleviate anxiety generated by emotionally precipitated illness, must retain his omnipotent stance. Should a patient be a doubting Thomas, something which is not at all unusual initially, the chances of the treatment being effective will be lessened. Using a series of exorcistic rituals which often include prescribing the tobacco mentioned earlier (which gives no visions but induces a feeling of non-ordinary reality), the healer can elaborate his treatment before the actual drug experience is undertaken. Prospective patients may then attend a few sessions in which others take ayahuasca in order to acquire an awareness or expectation of what people say happen to them under the drug.

To repeat an earlier point, the reappearance of certain elements in the drug experience by innumerable patients points to the important role that cultural expectations play. It is possible that the focus of the healer on a boa or another snake as the mother spirit of the vine which is beginning to heal or to anticipate healing by her appearance verifies and consolidates the magical learning that has taken place prior to the ayahuasca ingestion. Peoples' expectations that they will, in fact, be visited by such a boa or snake, as well as their belief in the curative prediction of success anticipated by that snake's appearance provides them with reassurance that healing is indeed occurring. In many ways, the omnipotence of the healer is increased by his symbolic presentations—his insistence upon the magical world of spirits or allies which he controls and that he can conjure up through his particular songs and incantations to appear before his patient. At sessions one often hears a healer advising his patient who is experiencing visions that the next song will cause a certain event to happen,

---

[3]Wolberg (1962: 173).

or that a difficult moment will pass, with pleasant visions to follow. The healer in many ways is conditioning the patients. Given a widely-shared belief system among members of the community and those versed in esoteric healing lore, these remarks of the healer must be seen in terms of their full impact upon the patient. Called upon as a creative source to interpret the symbols that may visually appear to a patient under his care, the healer sees in his patient's productions his own set of symbols, which he attributes to the magical causality of misfortune or disease.

This kind of occurrence, which Ehrenwald (1966), a medical historian, has called "doctrinal compliance," is important to consider in this context. In an interesting book tracing the continuity between present day scientific therapy and primitive healing, he coins this term to explain the fact that in Western therapy, despite the particular school of allegiance to which a psychiatrist may subscribe, his patient ends up doing what his doctor wants him to. If, for example, a healer is a Freudian, his patients' dreams tend to recreate early memories of childhood or family conflict. The patient in many ways complies with the therapist's unconscious wishes and expectations in order to validate his analyst's theories. Unlike the phenomenon of suggestion, which on the part of the therapist, at any rate, operates on a conscious level, doctrinal compliance seems to be an unconscious process, occurring in both magical and modern therapy procedures. This would seem to be the case in Peruvian healing with hallucinogens, since patients tend to see certain kinds of visions while under the effects of ayahuasca, after working with healers who share a common tradition of magical etiology.

Finally, Ludwig's comments on suggestibility are applicable here (1969: 17). He maintains that sensory overload, inherent in an hallucinogenic experience, can cause a person to attend most specifically to a guide's advice and counsel for reassurance in moments when he is in an altered state of consciousness.

## The Healer as Moral Arbiter of the Society

If we look at the kinds of health and social problems that the *ayahuasquero* treats, it is evident that much of his role is that of moral arbiter of society. This is especially so in light of the philosophy of causation which attributes illness and bad fortune to witchcraft. Not only is the healer's job to restore people to health, but he must take upon himself the omnipotent power and responsibility to punish evil doings. These healers who have made their moral commitment to paths of socially valued behavior often state they are deeply religious and will not perpetrate evil upon others. This contrasts, nonetheless, to their quickness to accept patients who believe they have been wronged. In the name of their patients, such men will not hesitate to punish others for their evil through the application of counter-magic. Although witches maintain that ayahuasca can give a man unlimited sexual access to women, nonetheless another important function of *ayahuasqueros* is to use their powers when under the drug to bring recalcitrant spouses who have strayed back to their homes once again.

As Herskovitz pointed out long ago (1946), Western dualistic categories of good and evil often do not properly convey non-literate and folk beliefs concerning magic. For example, although most *ayàhuasqueros* are called upon to heal patients who believe they have been bewitched, there is an element of true moral arbitration on the part of a healer who often uses counter magic to return evil to its perpetrator in order to relieve symptoms of illness. Easy categorization of good and evil does not adequately deal with the subtleties of ayahuasca use among Peruvian Mestizo populations in the rain forest region.

## Ayahuasca Healing and Psychotherapy

Perhaps the term psychotherapy is inadequate to describe and categorize the type of drug healing which is the subject of this book. This term is generally used in psychology to delineate a relationship between doctor and patient in which words play a very prominent part in the healing process. Although a certain amount of verbal exchange between healer and patient in the form of counseling, advising, suggesting, and exhorting does occur in Iquitos, many of the drug sessions described earlier are extremely subjective activities. The man or woman who takes the potion is left much to himself during the major part of the experience. As pointed out earlier, drug-adjuncted therapy in Western medicine employs much more directed verbal therapy.

Psychotherapy is seen by some as a learning process where new attitudes, feelings and behavior enter into a person's readaptation after he comes to a realization that his present way of life is distressing, ineffective, or damaging. Maladaptation marks the habits of a lifetime and must be changed in order for healing to occur. In considering the role that relearning plays in ayahuasca healing, we see that such therapy is of a short-term nature compared to the much longer periods of counseling involved in Western-type psychotherapy. Jungle patients may remain in treatment for only a week or two, with the longest periods of healing rarely running more than a few months in duration. The desire for the relief of symptoms seems to be the most pressing motivation for people to enter such sessions, accounting for the relatively short period of treatment time when compared to Euro-American psychological healing. Another factor should be taken into consideration. During my fieldwork in Belén, I constantly listened to complaints of physical illness, anxiety, lack of appetite, and the like, complaints comparable to those reported by other investigators working among urban poor throughout Peru. High rates of psychosomatic complaints characterize the life of the destitute poor throughout much of South America and some research even sees such stress as necessary for effective modernization (see Kellert *et al.,* 1967). When such daily stress and anxiety reaches intolerable levels, a person may look for help from a healer. Yet, we should keep in mind that the constant companion of many such people may be organic pain, discomfort, free-floating anxiety, general debility, and lack of energy coming from the many parasitical disorders with which they live. When such men and women finally find themselves in an ayahuasca session, they tend to look for relief of immediate problems. In speaking to both healers and patients, one rarely if ever hears these problems acknowledged to be personal maladjustment. Explaining illness as individual responsibility for misfortune or citing chance as a major factor does not occur. Rather, illness or misfortune is attributed to the evil of others—either malicious men and women who have brought magical harm, or else capricious, uncontrollable natural spirits that have punished a person who has violated a taboo.

Another important component of psychotherapy in Western medicine is the nature of the transference experience between a patient and his therapist, generally emerging after a reasonably long period of treatment. During this period, an emotional relationship to the therapist may be established, childhood memories may be recalled, abreaction of emotion may take place, and a new orientation for future living take place. As Freud wrote long ago, transference is usually described as the patient's tendency to see in his analyst the reincarnation of some important figure out of his childhood past, with the patient transferring to him feelings and reactions that undoubtedly applied to his model. In this way, the analyst may become the target of the patient's love or resentment which may have originally been directed to a parent.

In short-term ayahuasca healing, the mechanism of transference that is so important to theoretical conceptions of Western psychoanalysis is practically non-existent. It is quite true that healers tend to be older men or women who may have a relatively high status accorded them because of age, and who may serve as a parent-substitute. However, the short amount of time in which the patient is in treatment and the nature of the healing itself differ immensely from Western techniques we have been discussing.

As Kiev has pointed out (1968: 176), "the kind of illness that an individual has and how it may be treated is a function of his culture." The culture-specific methods used to reduce anxiety that characterize universally valid strategies throughout the world are no doubt enhanced by the properties of the hallucinogen itself. Reactions to both good and bad experiences—namely a feeling of relaxation, well-being, and ease with others can only reflect to the healer's benefit.

Ayahuasca is indeed a powerful hallucinogen that is used effectively in Peruvian rain forest healing. It has not been the purpose of this book to present statistics showing how many patients have been "cured" by this hallucinogen in emotional or psychological illness. Rather, it is hoped that the setting and background in which such healing takes place throws some light on the therapeutic potential of many different plant substances. In particular, the role of cultural variables such as beliefs, attitudes, and expectations in determining subjective experiences are important to stress. In some superficial ways, ayahuasca healing is comparable to Western techniques of psychotherapy, but such a comparison is doomed to an uncomfortable fit of theory with recalcitrant fact. The use of directed verbal interchange between therapist and patient in Euro-American society contrasts markedly with mechanisms of healing utilized in a society held together by a magical order of things.

## Conclusions

We have looked at the plant hallucinogen, ayahuasca, as an example of man's traditional use of such substances in the treatment of disease. As I pointed out at the beginning of this book, although it is convenient to separate out categories of drug use in which disease is viewed apart from supernatural concerns, it is important to reiterate here that ayahuasca healing in the Peruvian Amazon has very definite supernatural components of etiology, diagnosis, and cure as well as being viewed by healers and patients alike in terms of a philosophy of causation. The visions induced by the plant are interpreted by the ayahuasca healer to be the personal or spiritual force responsible for illness, a major concern prior to the effecting of any cure.

Although it is tempting to conclude that ayahuasca is functionally related to the social stresses and economic problems that beset members of the slum community and the jungle region today, one might hesitate to state that interpersonal strife is less now than it may have been or is presently among primitive populations in scattered rain forest villages. Perhaps a more convincing argument is that throughout time this powerful hallucinogen has been used in similar ways. Anxiety and stress, both today and in the past, can reach intolerable levels, so that a drug healer receives a call to ameliorate acute symptoms. In such situations of distress, ayahuasca has received its most varied elaboration—entering into the realm of tenuous, uneasy interpersonal relations and acting as a restorer of equilibrium in difficult situations.

# GLOSSARY

**Abrazo**    Embrace, clasp, hug. A common Peruvian form of greeting. This clasp at times is used to effect love magic, when a potion made from the dried genitals of a dolphin will be hidden on the arm or hand, and then the person to be bewitched will be touched in an *abrazo*.

**Agua florida**    Scented or perfumed water, used in healing sessions.

**Aguardiente**    Raw sugar cane rum.

**Ayahuasca,**

**Ayahuasquero**    Ayahuasca is the name used in Peru to describe several different species of *Banisteriopsis,* found in woody vines. These contain the alkaloids harmine and harmaline, which are responsible for the hallucinogenic effects. The most commonly used are *B. inebrians, B. rusbyana, B..quitensis* and *B. caapi. Ayahuasquero* is the name applied to folk healers who cure primarily emotional and psychological illness by using a potion prepared from boiling the ayahuasca vine.

**Barriada**    Spanish term used in Peru to describe urban squatter settlements, often illegally constituted, after a group of people suddenly appear on unused land and claim squatters' rights.

**Belén**    Name of the urban slum on the Amazon River in existence since the end of World War II. It is located in the south-east part of Iquitos and has an estimated 12,000 inhabitants.

**Brujo, Bruja**    A witch or evil-doer.

**Cantina**    Bar.

**Chacruna**    A plant used to prepare hallucinogenic brews. Believed to be *B. rusbyana* (containing Dimethyltryptamine).

**Chicha**    Fermented drink made from maize or other cereals.

**Cholo**    Civilized Indian. Term of derogation used to describe dark-skinned jungle transitional populations. Also used elsewhere in South America.

**Chonta**    A hardwood palm tree *(Euterpia edulis)* found in tropical South America. Indian groups believe that the chonta is an evil spirit which is introduced into the body of a person and causes illness. The only radical

141

cure for such illness is for a witch or healer to extract the thorn or spine from the sick person's body.

**Choza**    A hut or shack.

**Chullachaqui**    Quechua word signifying unequal feet. Refers to a mythological creature with one large foot and one small foot and a horrendous face. According to folk belief this creature stalks the forest and attracts incautious people to go into the woods with him, where he kills them.

**Cochinada**    Popular term for witchcraft potions made from the offal of vultures, river snakes, and the like. Used to cause one's enemies consistent bad luck or illness.

**Colectivo**    Motor powered wooden boats that carry passengers and cargo to and from market centers to outlying hamlets.

**Compadre**    Godfather; name given reciprocally by father and godfather of a child.

**Congonillo**    Odorific plant found in the rain forest, believed to be efficacious in love magic. One has only to wash one's spouse's clothing in a preparation made from the leaf to ensure that he will never leave home.

**Culebra**    Generic term for snake. The belief exists that a snake or boa constrictor is the mother-spirit of the hallucinogenic vine, ayahuasca, and appears to a person under the effects of the drug. If the person is able to dominate his fears, the snake then will show the person his special anayhuasca songs.

**Curioso**    Literally a curious person, but generally refers to a man or woman who possesses some general skill in healing or divining.

**Daño**    Harm, generally of a magical type, in which evil malice is held responsible for various kinds of illness.

**Despecho**    Ill will or a grudge seen as motivation for seeking out the services of a witch to cause harm to another.

**Empirico**    Synonymous with *curioso*.

**Ensalmo**    Spell, enchantment, or charm, believed to have been brought to the New World by Spanish conquerors and in particular adventurers who traveled throughout the coast of Peru practicing healing arts.

**Genios**    Allies, but in particular the spirits that a witch or *ayahuasquero* is believed to control, which he can use for either good or evil purposes.

**Gringa**    Nickname given to foreigners, especially English and Americans. Used frequently in Peru to mean light-skinned person in a non-pejorative.

**Huaco, Huaca**    Pottery vessel dating from prehistoric periods, believed efficacious in love magic in the North Coast of Peru. *Huaca* is the sacred shrine or grave site where such vessels are dug up.

**Icaros**    Witchcraft or healing orations, exorcisms, songs that have diverse ends. Some people perform *icaros* to be sure their friends do not betray them or that their enemies do not cause them *daño*.

**Loreto**   One of the twenty-five provinces of Peru. Iquitos is its capital city.

**Maestro**   Title of respect used to address an *ayahuasquero*.

**Mala vida**   Literally bad life. A common theme heard throughout the rain forest, referring to difficult relationships between men and women stemming in large part from extreme poverty.

**Mal de ojo**   Nervous illness resulting from the envious glance of one person upon another.

**Mapacho**   Mild tobacco found in Loreto and used in healing.

**Mareacíon**   Dizziness or non-ordinary state of reality initially experienced during hallucinogenic experience.

**Mesa**   Literally a table. Refers to the magical cloth laid out by coastal healers, some of whom use mescaline in their curing ritual.

**Mestizo**   Product of race mixing which has been taking place between Spanish and American Indians in South America since the early sixteenth century. Culturally speaking, a non-Indian.

**Monte**   Forest. Generally referred to as virgin jungle area without human habitation.

**Naipes**   Playing cards. In the rain forest region, a term applied to fortunetelling cards brought to South America by sixteenth century Spanish priests. The cards diffused to various regions of Peru and became incorporated into folk healing diagnostic practices.

**Psychedelic**   A term coined by Osmond (1957) referring to mind-manifesting qualities of certain psychotropic substances such as harmine, LSD, and mescaline.

**Pulsario**   A sickness delineated in the rain forest to designate nervousness, inability to remain still, and lack of tranquility. Mainly believed to affect women.

**Pusanga,**

**Pusanguero**   Originally a Brazilian word, it refers to a drink that is made from some herb, whose purpose is to inspire love in the heart of the person who drinks it. *Pusanguero* is the person skilled in such preparation.

**Quechua**   Indian language with over five million contemporary speakers found in the highlands of Peru, Ecuador, Bolivia, and Chile. Quechua spread to the Peruvian rain forest through missionary activity and has become incorporated into liturgical healing incantations.

**Regaton**   Commercial travelers who have large amounts of capital and travel through many jungle rivers selling staples to needy jungle farmers who often live in one-crop isolated hamlets.

**Rematista**   Small-scale, wholesaler of jungle produce; includes both men and women who resell their purchases in market centers.

**Saladera**   Illness consisting of constant bad luck in such areas as love, work, etc. Believed caused by witchcraft or sorcery on the part of an envious or vengeful person.

**St. Ciprian**   Catholic patron saint of folk healers throughout Peru.

**Sanitario**   Medical technicians, who are empirical healers who administer injections of penicillin or antibiotics to sick people. They are often poorly trained.

**Schacapa**   Indigenous name of a plant whose dried leaves are gathered together with a fiber and used as a rattle auxiliary in ayahuasca healing.

**Shaman**   Medicine man or witchdoctor.

**Shimi-Pampana**   Small, ordorless tuber used in love magic. The tuber is carefully chewed into a mash by the interested person, and then mixed with a fine perfume. It is believed that the herb will enable a girl to catch the man she loves.

**Sorcery**   The learning of magic for evil purposes; includes use of plant poisons and harmful substances.

**Susto**   Magical fright or soul loss, a folk illness commonly found throughout Peru and Latin America.

**Synesthesia**   Psychological term used to refer to the effects of mixing of various channels of sensory perception so that one channel interacts and substitutes for another. While under the effects of psychedelic drugs, for example, auditory sounds may be expressed visually.

**Tanrrilla**   Small, long-legged jungle bird used in love magic. When killed, the bird's hollow leg serves as a telescope through which a beloved is unknowingly viewed so that he will fall in love with the person effecting the charm.

**Tambo**   In the rain forest, a small, thatched shelter often without walls, used as a protection against the rain.

**Toé, Tohé**   Hallucinogenic plant, *Datura suavoleons* (of the *Solanaceous* family), mixed with other plants such as ayahuasca in preparing an infusion to be drunk.

**Trigueño**   Term used to describe brunette, light-brown-skinned people. An intermediate term between *moreno* (dark-skinned person) and *blanco* (white-skinned).

**Tunchis**   Birds who make prolonged whistle sounds. In Indian belief and among contemporary *Cholo* populations in the rain forest, these birds are thought to be the incarnation of some animal or human spirit that predicts great misfortune by its song. Also thought to be the departed spirits of the recent dead, retracing footsteps through the earth.

**Virote**   A dart believed sent magically by a witch to cause harm.

**Yacuruna**   Quechua word meaning water people. Mythical creature of the waters of rivers and lakes, a species of demon that causes many misfortunes.

**Yacumama**   Mother-spirit of the water, in Quechua. Often associated with the boa constrictor.

# BIBLIOGRAPHY

Abramson, Harold (ed.)
   1967   The Use of LSD in Psychotherapy and Alcoholism. New York: Bobbs-Merrill.

Alarco, R.
   1965   Analisis Musical de las Canciones del Ayahuasca, Usadas por los Brujos de la Tribu de los Orejones del Rio Napo y por los Curanderos de Iquitos. Informe. Lima.

Alexander, Franz
   1950   Psychosomatic Medicine: Its Principles and Applications. New York: Norton.

Anonymous
   n.d.   Cartomancía y Quiromancía: Adivinacíon del Presente y Porvenir por Medio de la Baraja Española. Lima.

Anonymous
   n.d.   La Mágia Negra y Arte Adivinatória. Mexico: Editorial Chapultepec.

Anonymous
   1957   La Mágia Blanca, Secreta y Adivinatória. Mexico: Editorial Juana de Arco.

Anonymous
   n.d.   La Mágia Verde o Amorosa. Mexico: Editorial Juana de Arco.

Anonymous
   n.d.   La Mágia Roja. Mexico: Editorial Juana de Arco.

Barber, Theodore X.
   1970   LSD, Marihuana, Hypnosis and Yoga. Chicago: Aldine Publishing Company.

Barret, P.
   1932   Le Yagé. Société des Americanistes de Paris XXIV:309–10

Blum, Richard et al.
   1969   Society and Drugs I. Stanford: Jossey-Bass, Inc.

Boiteau d'Ambly, D.
    1854    Les Cartes á Jouer et la Cartomancie. Paris: P. Jannet.
Bolinder, Gustaf
    1957    Indians on Horseback. London: D. Dobson.
Brooks, Jerome (ed.)
    1937    Tobacco, its History Illustrated by the Books, Manuscripts and
    Engravings in the Library of George Arents, Jr. Vol. I. New York: The
    Rosenbach Co.
Burroughs, William and Allen Ginsberg
    1963    The Yage Letters. San Francisco: City Light Books.
Caldwell, W.V.
    1968    LSD Psychotherapy: an Exploration of Psychedelic and Psy-
    cholytic Therapy. New York: Grove Press.
Cannon, Walter
    1942    Voodoo Death. American Anthropologist XLIV: 169–181.
Chagnon, Napoleon
    1968    Yanomamo: The Fierce People. New York: Holt, Rinehart, and
    Winston.
Cooper, J. M.
    1949    A Cross-Cultural Survey of South American Indian Tribes:
    Stimulants and Narcotics. In J. Steward (ed.), Handbook of South
    American Indians, Bureau of American Ethnology, Vol. 5, Bulletin 143,
    Washington, D. C.
Coriat, Juan E.
    1943    El Hombre del Amazonas y Ensayo Monografico de Loreto. 2nd
    Edition. Lima: Libreria Coriat.
Delay, Jean
    1967    Psychopharmacology and Psychiatry. Towards a Classification
    of Psychotropic Drugs. Bulletin on Narcotics 19: 1: 1-5. January.
Del Castillo, Gabriel
    1963    La Ayahuasca (sic). Planta Mágica de la Amazona. Perú In-
    digena 10: 24-25.
der Marderosian, A. H. et al.
    1968    Native Use and Occurrence of N-N-Dimethyltryptamine in the
    Leaves of Banisteriopsis rusbyana. American Journal of Pharmacy 140:
    5: 137–147, Sept. - Oct.
Diccionario de la Lengua Española
    1956    Royal Spanish Academy. Madrid.
Dobkin de Rios, Marlene
    1971    A Note on the Use of Ethno-tests and Western Projective Tests
    in a Peruvian Amazon Slum. Human Organization 30: 1: 89–94.
    1970    Banisteriopsis Used in Witchcraft and Healing Activities in

Iquitos, Peru. Economic Botany 24:35: 296–300.

1969a La Cultura de la Pobreza y la Mágia de Amor: Un Síndrome Urbano en la Selva Perúana. América Indígena XXIX:1 January.

1969b Curanderismo Psicodélico en el Perú: Continuidad y Cambio. Mesa Redonda de Ciencias Prehistóricas y Antropológicas. Instituto Riva Aguero. Universidad Católica del Perú. Lima.

1969c Fortune's Malice: Divination, Psychotherapy and Folk Medicine in Peru. Journal of American Folklore 82:324: 132–141.

1968 Folk Curing with a Psychedelic Cactus in N. Peru. International Journal of Social Psychiatry XV:1: 323–32. Fall-Winter.

Dobkin de Rios, Marlene
1984 Hallucinogens: Cross-Cultural Perspective. Albuquerque: University of New Mexico Press.

Dwarakanath, Shri C.
1965 The Use of Opium and Cannabis in the Traditional Systems of Medicine in India. Bulletin on Narcotics 17: 1: 15–19.

Ebin, David (ed.)
1961 The Drug Experience. New York: Grove Press.

Efron, David. (ed.)
1967 Ethnopharmacologic Search for Psychoactive Drugs. Public Health Service Publication No. 1645 National Institute of Mental Health. Washington, D.C.

Ehrenwald, Jan
1966 Psychotherapy: Myth or Method. New York: Grune and Stratton.

Eisner, Betty
1967 The Importance of the Non-Verbal. In Abramson, loc. cit.

Evans-Pritchard, E.
1937 Witchcraft, Oracles and Magic Among the Azande. Oxford: Clarendon Press.

Fort, Joel
1969 The Pleasure Seekers: The Drug Crisis, Youth and Society. New York: Grove Press.

Foster, George
1965 Peasant Society and the Image of Limited Good. American Anthropologist 67: 298–315.

Friedberg, Claudine
1965 Des Banisteriopsis utilises comme Drogue en Amerique du Sud. Journal d'Agriculture Tropicale et de Botanique Appliquée XII, 9–12, Sept. - Dec., Paris.

1959 Rapport sur une Mission au Perou-Description du Materiel

Recueilli, Exposé, Sommaire des Recherches Enterprises. Travaux de l'Institut Francais d'Etudes Andines 7: 65.

Fuentes, Hildebrando
    1908   Loreto: Apuntes Geográficos, Históricos, Estadísticos, Políticos y Sociales. Lima: Ediciones Popular Selva.

Fuenzalida, Fernando *et al.*
    1970   El Indio y el Poder en el Perú. Instituto de Estudios Perúanos. Lima: Moncloa-Campodonico.

Garcilaso de la Vega
    1961   The Royal Commentaries of the Inca. New York: Avon Books.

Gebelin, Court de M.
    1781   Monde Primitif, Analysé et Comparé avec le Monde Moderne. Vol. 8. Paris: C. C. Meyrueis.

Giraldo, Pineda
    1950   Aspectos de la Mágia en la Guajiro. Revista del Instituto Etnológica Nacional, Bogota.

Girard, R.
    1958   Indios Selváticos de la Amazonía Perúana. Mexico: Libro Mexicano.

Goldman, Irving
    1963   The Cubeo. Indians of the Northwest Amazon. Illinois Studies in Anthropology, No. 2, Urbana.

Grajeda, O.
    1964   Estudio Socio-económico de Belén. Universidad Nacional de la Amazonía Perúana. Iquitos.

Gutierrez-Noriega, Carlos
    1950   Area de Mescalinismo en el Perú. América Indígena 10: 215.

Hambling, J.
    1965   Are Guilt and Anxiety Experienced Differently from Patients Suffering from Psychoneurotic and Psychosomatic Illness? In J. Wisdom and H. Wolff (eds.), the Role of Psychosomatic Disorder in Adult Life. New York: Pergamon Press.

Harner, Michael J.
    1968   The Sound of Rushing Water. Natural History LXXVII: 6, June - July.
    1962   Jivaro Souls. American Anthropologist 64:258–272.

Heim, Roger
    1969   Les Champignons Toxiques et Hallucinogènes. Paris: Editions du Museum National d'Histoire Naturelle.

Hernandez, Arturo
    1960   Bubinzana, la Canción Magica del Amazonas. Lima: Imprenta del Ministerio de Guerra.

Herrera, Jenaro
1965 Las Amazonas (Leyendas y Tradiciones de Loreto). Iquitos: Ediciones Popular Selva.
Herskovitz, Melville J.
1946 Man and His Works. New York: Alfred A. Knopf.
Hoffer, A. *et al.*
1967 The Hallucinogens. New York: Academic Press.
Janiger, Oscar and Marlene Dobkin de Rios
n.d. Suggestive Hallucinogenic Properties of Tobacco. Manuscript.
Karsten, Rafael
1923 Blood Revenge, War and Victory Feasts among the Jibaro Indians of Eastern Ecuador. Smithsonian Institution, Bureau of American Ethnology, Bulletin 79, Washington, D.C.
1935 Headhunters of the Western Amazonas. Life and Culture of Jibaro Indians of E. Ecuador and Peru. Societas Scientarum Fennica, Vol. 7, Helsingfors.
Katz, Fred and Marlene Dobkin de Rios
1971 Hallucinogenic Music: an Analysis of the Role of Whistling in Peruvian Ayahuasca Healing Sessions. Journal of American Folklore (in press).
Kellert, Stephen *et al.*
1967 Culture Change and Stress in Rural Peru: A Preliminary Report. Milbank Memorial Fund Quarterly XLV:4, October.
Kennedy, John G.
1970 Psycho-social Dynamics of Witchcraft Systems. International Journal of Social Psychiatry 90.
Kensinger, Kenneth M. *et al.*
1970 The Use and Hallucinatory Principles of a Psychoactive Beverage of the Cashinahua Tribe (Amazon Basin). Drug Dependence, National Institute of Mental Health, Washington, D.C., October.
Kiev, Ari
1968 Curanderismo. New York: Free Press.
Kilson, Marion
1968 A Note on Trance Possession Among the Ga of Western Ghana. Transcultural Psychiatric Research V, April.
Kluckhohn, Clyde
1944 Navaho Witchcraft. Boston: Beacon Press.
Koch-Grunberg, T.
1908 Die Hianokoto: umaua. Antropos 3:83: 124; 297–33; 924–28.
Kroeber, Alfred
1948 Anthropology. New York: Harcourt, Brace.

LaBarre, Weston
   1970   Old and New World Narcotics: a Statistical Question and an
   Ethnological Reply. Economic Botany 24:1: 73–80. January - March.
   1964   The Peyote Cult. Hamden, Conn: Shoe String Press.
Larson, Magali *et al.*
   1969   Social Stratification in Peru. Politics of Modernization. Series
   No. 5. Institute of International Studies, Berkeley.
Lastres, Juan
   1956   La Medicina en el Descubrimiento y Conquista del Perú. Universidad Nacional Mayor de San Marcos, Lima.
   1951   História de la Medicina Perúana. Vol. 1, La Medicina Incáica.
   Universidad Nacional Mayor de San Marcos, Lima.
Lathrap, Donald
   1970   Alternative Models of Population Movement in the Tropical
   Lowlands of South America. Paper read at 39th International Congress
   of Americanists, Aug. 6, 1970, Lima.
Lemlij, M. *et al.*
   1965   Del Uso de Psicodisléptico en la Selva Perúana. In Perú, Sanidad
   del Gobierno y Policía. Universidad Nacional Mayor de San Marcos,
   Lima.
Lenormand, M.
   n.d.   El Arte de Echar las Cartas. La Cartomancia y Quiromancia.
   Mexico: Ediciones Chapultepec.
Levi, Eliphas (Pseudonym)
   1938   Transcendental Magic, its Doctrine and Ritual, by Alphonse
   Louis Constant. Translated by Arthur Waite. London: Paternoster
   House.
Lewin, Louis
   1964   Phantastica: Narcotic and Stimulating Drugs, Their Use and
   Abuse. 2nd Edition. New York: E. P. Dutton and Company, Inc.
Lewis, Oscar
   1966   La Vida. New York: Random House.
Lowie, Robert
   1949   Introduction. The Tropical Rain Forest. In Julian Steward, ed.,
   Handbook of South American Indians. Volume 3, The Tropical Forest
   Tribes. Smithsonian Institution, Bulletin 143, Washington, D.C.
Ludwig, Arnold M.
   1969   Altered States of Consciousness. In Charles Tart (ed.), Altered
   States of Consciousness. New York: John Wiley and Sons, Inc.
Masters, R. and Jean Houston
   1966   The Varieties of Psychedelic Experience. New York: Delta.

Matos, Jose (ed.)
1968 La Dominacíon de América Latina. Instituto de Estudios Perúanos. Lima: Ediciones Moncloa.

McGlothlin, William
1967 Social and Para-Medical Aspects of Hallucinogenic Drugs. In Abramson (ed.), *op. cit.*

Naranjo, Claudio
1967 Psychotropic Properties of the Harmala Alkaloids. In Daniel Efron (ed.), The Ethnopharmacologic Search for Psychoactive Drugs. Public Health Service Publication No. 1645. National Institute of Mental Health, Washington, D.C.

Naranjo, Plutarco
1968 Plantas Psicotrópicas de America y Bioquimica de la Mente. Paper read at the 5th Latin American Congress of Psychiatry, Bogotá, Colombia.

Osmond, Humphry
1957 A Review of the Clinical Effects of Psychotomimetic Agents. Annals of the New York Academy of Science 66:418–34.

Oviedo, Jesus *et al.*
1964 Estudio Socio-económico de la Barriada del Puerto de Belén de la Ciudad de Iquitos. Escuela de Servicio Social, Lima.

Papus (Pseudonym)
1891 Traite Methodique de Magie Pratique par Gerard Encausse. Paris: Librairie Generale des Sciences Occultes.

Park, George
1967 Divination and its Social Context. In J. Middleton (ed.), Magic, Witchcraft and Curing. New York: Doubleday.

Perez de Barradas, Jose
1950 Drogas Ilusionogénicas de los Indios Americanos. Anthropología y Etnología 3: 9–107.

Pinedo, Victor
1966 Evaluacíon Económica de los Recursos Ictiológicos de la Amazonía Perúana. Universidad Nacional Mayor de San Marcos. Lima.

Plog, Stanley C. and Robert S. Edgerton (eds.)
1969 Changing Perspectives in Mental Illness. New York: Holt, Rinehart, and Winston.

Pope, Harrison G.
1969 *Tabernanthe Iboga:* an African Narcotic Plant of Social Importance. Economic Botany 23: 2: 174–184.

Prince, Raymond (ed.)
1969 Do Psychedelic Drugs have Religions Significance? Proceedings,

3rd Annual Conference, R.M. Bucke Society, McGill University, Montreal, Canada.

Ramirez, Juan
    1963    Yacuruna. Ministerio de Educacíon Pública. Iquitos.
Rios Reategui, Oscar
    1962    Aspectos Preliminares al Estudio Farmaco-Psiquiátrico del Ayahuasca y su Principio Activo. Anales de la Facultad de Medicina. Universidad Nacional Mayor de San Marcos. Lima, Peru.
Roessner, Tomas
    1946    El Ayahuasca. Planta Magica del Amazonas. Revista Geografica Americana. Buenos Aires 29: 14-16.
Schultes, Richard Evans
    1970    The Plant Kingdom and Hallucinogens (part III). Bulletin on Narcotics XXII:1: 24–52.
    1969    The Unfolding Panorama of the New World Hallucinogens. In J. Guenckel (ed.), Current Topics in Plant Science. New York: Academic Press.
    1967    The Place of Ethnobotany in the Ethnopharmacologic Search for Psychotomimetic Drugs. In D. Efron (ed), Ethnopharmacologic Search for Psychoactive Drugs. Public Health Service Publication 1645, National Institute of Mental Health, Washington, D.C.
    1965    Botanical Sources of New World Narcotics. In G. Weil (ed.), Psychedelic Reader, New York: University Books.
    1957    The Identity of Malpighiaceous Narcotics of South America. Harvard University Botanical Museum Leaflets 18:1, June.
Seguín, Carlos Alberto
    1970    Folklore Psychiatry. In S. Arieti (ed.), The World Biennial of Psychiatry and Psychotherapy. Vol. I. New York: Basic Books.
Segura, Manuel and Helena Sanjaman
    1956    Cartomancia. Barcelona: Editorial Ruperto Diaz.
Seitz, Georg J.
    1967    Epená, the Intoxicating Snuff Powder of the Waika Indians and the Tucano Medicine Man, Agostino. In D. Efron, loc. cit.
Silva, Max et al.
    1965    El Curanderismo en Lima. Revista de Ciencias Psicológicas y Neurológicas 2: 1: 16-49.
Singer, Samuel W.
    1816    Researches into the History of Playing Cards. London: R. Triphook.
Siskind, Janet
    1972    Preliminary Report of an Investigation of the use of Ayahuasca

by a Tribe of the Selva. In M. Harner (ed.), Hallucinogens and Shamanism (in press).

Spence, Lewis
    1920    An Encyclopedia of Occultism. New York: University Books.

Spruce, Richard
    1908    Notes of a Botanist on the Amazon and Andes. Vol. 2. London: MacMillan.

Steward, Julian H. and Louis Faron
    1959    Native Peoples of South America. New York: McGraw Hill.

Tart, Charles T.
    1969    Altered States of Consciousness. New York: John Wiley and Sons, Inc.

Taylor, Norman
    1966    Narcotics: Nature's Dangerous Gifts. New York: Dell.

Tovar, Enrique D.
    1966    Vocabulario del Oriente Perúana. Universidad Nacional Mayor de San Marcos. Lima.

Universidad Nacional Mayor de San Marcos
    1964    La Poblacíon del Llano Amazónico (Depto. de Loreto). Instituto General de Investigacíon. October.

Valdivia, Oscar
    1964    Historía de la Psiquiatría Perúana. Universidad Nacional Mayor de San Marcos. Lima.

Van Rijnberk, Gerard
    1947    Le Tarot, Histoire, Inconographie, Esoterisme. Lyon: P. Derain.

Varese, Stefano
    1970    Las Minorías Étnicas de la Moñtana Perúana. Esquema para una Antropología de Urgencia. Universidad Nacional Mayor de San Marcos, Facultad de Letras y Ciéncias Humanas. Lima.

Villavicencio M.
    1858    Geography of the Republic of Ecuador. New York: Graighead.

Walkington, David L. et al.
    1960    Antibiotic Activity of an Extract of Peyote (Lophophora Williamsii (lemaire) Coulter). Economic Botany 14:3: 247–249. July - Sept.

Wasson, R.G. and V.P. Wasson
    1957    Russia, Mushrooms and History, 2 volumes. New York: Pantheon Books.

Weiss, Edward and O. English
    1957    Psychosomatic Medicine. Philadelphia: Saunders.

Whiffen, Thomas
    1915    The Northwest Amazonas: Notes of Some Months Spent Among
    Cannibal Tribes. London: Constable.
Wils, Frits
    1968    Estudio Sobre Iquitos—Para un Plan Regulador. Oficina Na-
    cional de Planeamento y Urbanismo de Lima. CISEPSA, Lima.
    1967    Estudio Social sobre Belén—Iquitos. Centro de Investigaciones
    Sociales, Económicas, Políticas y Antropológicas. Lima.
Wolberg, Lewis R.
    1966    Psychotherapy and the Behavioral Sciences. New York: Grune
    and Stratton.

# Index

Acculturation, 53 ff.

Acosta, José de, 30

*Auga Florida,* 31

Aguardiente, 108

  *See also* Alcohol

Alcohol, Alcoholism, 2, 16, 34, 87, 108

Alkaloids of Ayahuasca, 20, 22

Amazon region:

  description of, 7, 43–45

  history of, 49 ff., 54

Andean area, comparison with rain forest, 54

Ayahuasca:

  botany of, 8, 20, 43

  chemistry of, 22, 133

  cultural conditioning and, 136–137

  diets connected with, 72, 102, 111, 118

  dosage level of, 71, 120

  in divination, 45

  effects of, 8, 68, 75, 97, 128, 133

  etymology of, 43, 46

  healing sessions, description of, 8, 68, 69–76, 105, 132

  love magic and, 64, 113, 135, 138

  as medicine, 132, 129, 134

  mother spirit of, 115, 118–119

  music, use of, 23, 69, 72, 73, 118, 120, 131–133, 136–137

  patients, 7–8, 67, 107 ff.

  Peruvian law and, 69

  placebo effects of, 133

  pleasure and social interaction, 45

  primitive use of, 19, 43–47, 120

  psychotherapy and, 7, 131, 136

  the supernatural and, 45, 46

  synonyms for, 43, 46

  the treatment of disease and, 45, 47, 111, 129

  use, and cultural variables effecting, 9, 121, 140

  use, in folklore, 94

  visions, 117–128

  vomiting, induced by, 68, 71, 73

*Ayahuasquero:*

  apprentices and, 75, 106

  biographies of, 99–107

  characteristics of, 113–114

  as charlatan, 136–137

  diagnostic procedures, 88, 114, 118

  expectation of disease etiology, 134, 137

  fear of police, 114

  fees for healing, 82, 106–107

  as guru, 133, 137

  healing techniques, 68, 72–76, 82, 86, 129–131, 134, 136

  as moral arbiter, 108, 137–138

  omnipotence of, 134–137

  selection of, by patient, 67, 113

  selection of patients, 67–68, 130

*Banisteriopsis,* 8, 20, 43

  *See also* Ayahuasca

Barber, Theodore, 22

*Barriada; see* Slum

Belén:

  description of, 9 ff.

  economic and social decay of, 10, 58

  family instability in, 59, 61

  household composition of, 59

  marital tension in, 61

  occupations in, 51, 58–59, 62

origins of, 55
pathology in, 58 ff.
population of, 9
social structure of, 51–53, 58 ff., 61, 82–83, 115
  *See also* Slums
Blum, Richard, 37
Brujo; see *Witches*
Bwiti, Bouiti, 31

Caldwell, W. 131
Cashinahua use of Ayahuasca, 120
*Chacruna (B. Rusbyana),* 100, 130
Children, activities of in Belén, 59–60
Cholification process, 53 ff.
*Cholo:*
  barriers to social integration of, 53, 56–57
  contrasted to Mestizo, 52–53, 82
  definition of, 51, 54
  racial characteristics of, 51, 55
Chonta, 46, 75
Coca, 34
*Colectivo,* 108
*Congonillo,* 63
Consciousness, altered states of:
  adaptive/maladaptive dimensions of, 25
  ayahuasca and, 9
  characteristics of, 23–24
  hallucinogens and, 19
  non-drug induced, 23
Creole, 56
Cubeo, use of poisonous plants, 96
*Culebra,* 118
"Culture of Poverty," 59, 62
Curandero; *see* Folk healer
Curing; *see* Folk healing, Healing
*Curioso,* 12, 64, 92.
  *See also* Folk healer

*Daño,* 85–86, 92, 102, 104, 106, 112
*Datura,* 33, 69, 104, 111, 130
Delay, Jean, 22
de Rios, Marlene Dobkin; *see* Dobkin de Rios, Marlene
*Despecho,* 87
Diet, in Iquitos, 57, 59
Disease; *see* Illness
Divination; *see* Fortunetelling, *Naipes*
Dobkin de Rios, Marlene, ayahuasca visions of, 125–126
Doctrinal compliance, 137

Dolphins and magic, 79, 81
Drugs:
  pleasure and social interaction, 34 ff.
  the supernatural and, 29 ff.
  the treatment of disease and, 31 ff.
  *See also* Hallucinogens, Psychedelics, *and* Psychotropic drugs

Economy:
  in Iquitos, 49, 51
  subsistence, 58 ff.
Education:
  quality of in slum, 60
Ehrenwald, Jan, 137
Eisner, Betty, 131
El Dorado, 49–50
Empírico, 65
  *See also* Folk healer
Ensalmo, 77
*Epená:*
  use in Venezuela, 34
Euro-American influences in Iquitos, 7, 58
Evans-Pritchard, E., 96
Evil eye; *see Mal de ojo*
Exploitation of poor in Belén, 55 ff.

Fishing in Belén, 59
Fly agaric, 30
Folk healers:
  omnipotence of, 134–137
  psychosomatic disorders and, 91, 97
  search for, 67
  techniques of curing, 68, 72–76, 82, 86, 92, 97, 129–131, 134, 136, 140
  *See also Curioso, Curandero, and Ayahuasquero*
Folk healing:
  mechanisms of, with ayahuasca, 129–140
  rituals of, with ayahuasca, 8, 68, 69, 70 ff.
Folklore, 79–82
  Chullachaqui, 79
  snakes in, 56, 118, 136
  Tunchis, 79
  Yacumama, 79
  Yacuruna, 79
Folk medicine, 32–33
  magical conditioning and exorcism, 136
  *See also* Folk healers
Fort, Joel, 28
Fortunetelling:

as anthropological field technique, 12–13, 93, 115
diagnostic uses of, 88–89
history in Latin America, 89, 91
*See also Naipes*
Funeral Customs, 131

Ginsberg, Allen, 123–124
Girard, R. 46
Grajeda, O., 15, 56
Guien, M. 31

Hakula spirits, 35
Hallucinogens:
definition of, 20, 22
as drugs of awareness, 22, 23
effects of mixing various, 69, 130–131
*Epená*, 34
historical examples of use of, 26 ff.
human evolution and, 26
maladaptive/adaptive aspects of, 28, 43
pleasure and social interaction in use of, 42
the supernatural and, 29, 33, 37 ff.
the treatment of disease and, 34, 141
use in North American society, 25
use in South American society, 20, 34, 37 ff.
witchcraft and, 37, 43
*See also* Psychedelics, Ayahuasca, Marijuana, *Yagé, Chacruna, Datura, Toé,* Fly agaric
Harmine; *see* Ayahuasca, Alkaloids of Ayahuasca
Harner, Michael, 45–46, 121–122
Healing; *see* Folk healing
Hoffer, A., 22
Hookworm, 57

Iboga, use in west Africa, 31
*Icaros,* 130
Illness:
case histories of, 84–88, 111
emotional and psychological, 88, 91–92, 139
etiology of, 54, 57, 64, 78–79, 86, 103, 111, 129, 134
folk categories of, 78–79, 84–88, 139
Institute of Social Psychiatry, Lima, 8, 104
Iquitos:
description of, 7, 9, 51
ethnography of, 49 ff., 58 ff.
history of, 49 ff.

Katz, Fred, 133

Kennedy, John G., 43, 97
Kensinger, Kenneth, 120
Kilson, Marion, 23

La Barre, Weston, 28
*La mala vida,* 61
Lastres, Juan, 77
Lathrap, D., 53
Lewis, Oscar, 59
Loreto, 50
Love magic:
described, 10, 12, 62–64, 81
world view and, 62, 65
LSD:
author's experience and, 125–126
psychotherapy and, 22, 132–133
Ludwig, Arnold, 23–24, 137

Magic, 7, 49, 109, 128, 134, 138, 140
*Mal de ojo,* 87
Malnutrition in Belén, 57
Marijuana, 33
Marriage:
adultery and, 61–62
breakup of, 59, 61
forms of, 61
Matos, José, 57
Mazatec drug use, 30
Masters, R., 133
Medicine, western in Iquitos, 47, 82
Menstruation, taboos on, 79, 107
Mescaline, 32–33
Mestizo, 19, 53–54
Migration:
within Amazon region, 55–56
by Europeans in rubber epoch, 50
Mushrooms, hallucinogenic, 29–31
Music; *see* Ayahuasca and music

*Naipes:*
history of, 89–91
diagnosis of illness and, 92–93
field technique and, 12–13, 89, 93, 115
Naranjo, Claudio, 122
Narcotics, 22
Native American Church, 33

Oviedo, Jesus, 60
*Ololiuqui,* 30
Osmond, H., 22

Peasants:

in cities, 58 ff.
in rural areas, 14–15
*Petun,* 30
Peyote, 33–34
Photography:
  field technique and, 13–14
  in witchcraft, 13
Pituri, use by Australian aborigines, 34
Pope, H., 31
Poverty in Belén, 56, 58
Psychedelic experience:
  characteristics of, 20
  dosage level, 23
  evidence for antiquity of use, 26 ff.
  factors contributing to, 22
  HRAF study of, 37
  longitudinal dangers of, 43
  use in South America, 19–20, 33–34, 37 ff.
Psychosomatic illness, 88, 91, 134–135, 139–
  140
Psychotropic drugs:
  history of, 28 ff.
  properties of, 20–22
  *See also* Hallucinogens, Psychedelics
*Pulsario,* 87
*Pusanga,* 93

Quechua, 72

*Regaton,* characteristics of, 59
Reinburg, P., 45
Religion:
  music used in ceremonies of, 131
  Roman Catholic influences in Belén, 55, 77,
    105, 107
  Roman Catholic influences in Peruvian
    coast, 33
*Rematista,* 58, 62
Rios Reategui, Oscar, 91, 114, 115
Rubber epoch, 50, 55–56
Rumrrill, Roger, 2–5, 58

St. Ciprian, 104
*Saladera,* 86, 108, 133
Salt, 72, 102, 111, 118
*Sanitarios,* 78
*San Pedro,* 8, 32–33
*Schacapa* rattle, 72, 73
Schultes, Richard, 31, 43, 124
Seguin, Carlos Alberto, 8, 68, 114
Sexual relations:

between spouses, 63, 109
exploitation of women, 57
expressed in love magic, 62–64
extramarital, 61–62
values of premarital chastity, 53, 59
Shaman, 54
  *See also Ayahuasquero*
Sharanahua, use of Ayahuasca, 47
*Shimi-pampana,* 63
Siskind, Janet, 47
Slums:
  Cholo-Mestizo relationships, 52–53
  discrimination against residents of, 57
  economic and social decay of, 9 ff., 62, 65
  family instability, 60–61, 62
  housing decay, 9 ff.
  pathology in, 9 ff., 60, 62, 65
  psychosomatic illness in, 139–140
  sexual behavior in, 59
  underemployment, 51, 58
  *See also* Belén
Snakes; *see* Folklore, snakes in
Social classes:
  conflict between, 82–83
  elites, 53
  stratification, 51–53
  *trigueño,* 51
Social control:
  gossip as, 62
  *See also* Witchcraft
Sociological surveys:
  of Belén, 15 ff., 56
  of Iquitos, 15
Sorcery; *see* Witchcraft
Spanish view of native medicine, 77–78
Spruce, Richard, 121
*Susto,* 84, 92

*Tambo,* 69, 76
*Tanrrilla,* 63
Tarot cards, 91
*Teonanactl,* Aztec use of, 30
Tobacco, 8, 28, 34, 69, 72, 104, 107, 130–131,
  136
*Trigueños,* 51
*Tunchis,* 79

Varese, Stéfano, 55
Visions:
  Amazonian informants, 112, 113
  ayahuasca and, 117–120

expectations of and healing, 136–137
western observers and ayahuasca, 120–128

Walkington, D., 33
Wasson, R. G. and V. P., 26
Wils, Frits, 15
Witchcraft:
  belief in, 95
  death and, 95
  functional/dysfunctional aspects of, 96–97
  illness and, 77 ff.
  paranoid delusions and, 97

Spanish influence on indigenous patterns of
  77
Witches:
  ayahuasca and, 93–96
  characteristics of, 87, 94, 95
  in folklore, 94
Women, in Belén, 57–58 ff., 61–62

*Yaje, Yage,* 121

Zaparo Indians use of ayahuasca, 45